W9-BIP-331

REFUGE

—FROM THE—

STORM

LIVING IN THE LAST DAYS

REFUGE
— FROM THE —
STORM

CRAIG JAMES OSTLER

Covenant Communications, Inc.

Cover image right to left: *The Moon* © Digital Vision courtesy of Getty Images, *Salt Lake Temple* © Ken Zirkel courtesy of istockphoto.com, *Jerusalem* © 5Craig James Ostler.

Cover design copyright © 2012 by Covenant Communications, Inc.

Published by Covenant Communications, Inc.
American Fork, Utah

Copyright © 2012 by Craig James Ostler
Copyright © of General Authority quotes by Intellectual Reserve, Inc.

All rights reserved. No part of this book may be reproduced in any format or in any medium without the written permission of the publisher, Covenant Communications, Inc., P.O. Box 416, American Fork, UT 84003. This work is not an official publication of The Church of Jesus Christ of Latter-day Saints. The views expressed within this work are the sole responsibility of the author and do not necessarily reflect the position of The Church of Jesus Christ of Latter-day Saints, Covenant Communications, Inc., or any other entity.

Printed in Canada
First Printing: August 2012

18 17 16 15 14 13 12   10 9 8 7 6 5 4 3 2 1

ISBN 978-1-60861-323-6

Acknowledgments

I IMAGINE THAT MANY AUTHORS approach their works with great enthusiasm and then need encouragement and help along the way to make their efforts a reality. My case is especially true in the welcomed reassurance and support I have received. First, I acknowledge the loving motivation and inspiration from my sweet wife, Sandy. Her faith in me stands supreme above any other considerations on earth. All of my children have expressed support for my writing, but I am thankful for the special interest my son Derek has shown and how constantly he has inquired about how I am coming along with this work. Again, my parents and siblings are always supportive, but I am especially grateful for the many conversations I have had with my brother Jeff about the last days and the Savior's Second Coming. I have also felt heavenly support and attentiveness, even from my dear grandmother Mary Myrtle Bodell Ostler, with whom, among others, I expect to rejoice in the day of the Lord when the righteous are raised from their graves and caught up with those on earth to meet the Savior as He descends from the clouds of heaven in glory. In no way do these individuals bear any responsibility for what I have written; in some cases they may not even agree, but their support has been unwavering.

I received notable and helpful suggestions from my friend and colleague Richard D. Draper, and Samantha Van Walraven and her staff at Covenant Communications. I teased Samantha that her contributions and editing should qualify her as a coauthor of this book. For their tireless efforts in tracking down original sources, I also thank my student assistants: Ryan Chapman, Amanda Christensen, and Katie Parker. Last, I am grateful for the many students at BYU, in the adult religion classes, and in my early seminary teaching years who have asked questions and given me fire for teaching from the scriptures and the words of modern apostles and prophets.

TABLE OF CONTENTS

INTRODUCTION

This volume was written with the knowledge and understanding that the clearest and most accurate information regarding the last days and Christ's return to the earth is provided in the scriptures and the teachings of latter-day prophets.

WHEN I WAS COMMISSIONED TO write this book, I asked, "Have not enough books been written on the last days, the signs of the times, and the Second Coming?" Thirty years ago, I devoured Elder Bruce R. McConkie's volume *The Millennial Messiah.* Gerald Lund compiled many statements from modern general authorities in *The Coming of the Lord.* My friend and colleague Richard D. Draper penned *The Savior's Prophecies: From the Fall of Jerusalem to the Second Coming.* In addition, Joseph Fielding McConkie and I wrote commentary on all of the modern revelations regarding this topic within our volume *Revelations of the Restoration: A Commentary on the Doctrine and Covenants and Other Modern Revelations.* What might I add to those that have taken up this task before me or add to what I had already written? However, I felt uplifted as I determined to provide a vision of the last days in a simplified fashion and to include a broader perspective of those who have lived in the last days, from the time of the Prophet Joseph Smith until now.

One of the challenges for any student of the scriptures studying the signs of the times and the Second Coming is to deal with statements past Church leaders made that seemed to indicate that the Second Coming was imminent. Thus, in this volume, I have explained to the best of my understanding why LDS leaders and members may have thought that they lived in a time in which the coming of Christ surely was but a short time away. Many believed, and even taught others, that they would live to see the Savior return, yet they died without the sight. A brief discussion of historical context in those times adds light to their thinking.

Most importantly, I have a few objectives that I hope will benefit the readers: first, that they will have accurate information; second, that their testimonies will increase of the truthfulness of the words of the prophets as they see prophecies of the last days fulfilled; third, that they will have confidence in being prepared to live in the last days; fourth, that they will see their part in helping others during times of prophesied tribulation; and fifth, that they will rejoice in looking forward to the time of the Savior's Second Coming.

The Lord Jesus Christ has assured His disciples in all ages that He will return to the earth in glory in the latter days to usher in the promised Millennium. The record of those assurances is found in the scriptures and teachings of the Lord's servants, the prophets. In this volume, I invite you to search the scriptures and prophetic teachings regarding the Savior's appearances at Adam-ondi-Ahman and Mount Zion, upon the Mount of Olives, and to the world and become better acquainted with signs that will attend the Lord's glorious return to the earth. The Lord may not have revealed every detail concerning the last days and His appearances, but He has provided sufficient information to help His Saints prepare for and anticipate them. Once you learn more about the prophetic word concerning the Lord's coming, you may well declare in your heart, as did Alma concerning the Savior's first coming, "Would to God that it might be in my day; but let it be sooner or later, in it I will rejoice" (Alma 13:25).

The Lord's Outline of the Last Days and the Second Coming (D&C 87; 88:87–101)

The Lord revealed a basic outline of the future to the Prophet Joseph Smith in two revelations given within a few days of each other. The first, a revelation and prophecy on war, came on Christmas Day 1832 (see D&C 87). Two days later, the Lord revealed what has become known as the "Olive Leaf" revelation (see D&C 88).[1] These two revelations serve as an appropriate introduction to the last days and the Second Coming. True, they are a brief outline in comparison to other revelations that provide greater detail regarding specific aspects of these topics, but such an overview helps us have something to build upon as we study and consider additional revelations that have addressed the last days. In bullet point form, the events include:

- Civil War will occur between the Northern states and the Southern states (D&C 87:3)

- "War shall be poured out on all nations" (D&C 87:3)

- "Slaves shall rise up against their masters" (D&C 87:4)

- "Remnants . . . will marshal themselves . . . and vex the Gentiles" (D&C 87:5)

- War, bloodshed, famine, plagues, earthquakes, waves of the sea, and lightning will chasten the inhabitants of the earth until they have "made a full end of all nations" (D&C 87:6; 88:87, 90)

- The sun will be darkened, the moon "bathed in blood," and stars fall (D&C 88:87)

- "All things shall be in commotion" (D&C 88:91)

- "Men's hearts shall fail," and people will fear (D&C 88:91)

- The Saints will gather and "stand . . . in holy places" (D&C 87:8)

- A great sign will appear in heaven (D&C 88:93)

- The wicked will be readied to be burned as tares in a field (D&C 88:94)

- The Saints who are alive on earth will be quickened and caught up to meet Christ (D&C 88:96)

- The righteous dead will resurrect and "be caught up to meet [Christ]" (D&C 88:97)

- The wicked will remain unresurrected in the spirit world (D&C 88:100–101)

The Prophet Joseph Smith wrote:

> The earth will soon be reaped—that is, the wicked must soon be destroyed from off the face of the earth, for the Lord hath spoken it, and who can stay the hand of the Lord, or who is there that can measure arms with the Almighty, for at his commands the heavens and the earth must pass away. The day is fast hastening on when the restoration of all things shall be fulfilled, which all the holy prophets have

prophesied of, even unto the gathering in of the house of Israel. Then shall come to pass that the lion shall lie down with the lamb, etc.

But, brethren, be not discouraged when we tell you of perilous times, for they must shortly come, for the sword, famine, and pestilence are approaching. There shall be great destructions upon the face of this land, for ye need not suppose that one jot or tittle of the prophecies of all the holy prophets shall fail, and there are many that remain to be fulfilled yet. The Lord hath said that a short work will he make of it, and the righteous shall be saved if it be as by fire.[2]

One of the purposes of this volume is to make you think. Even after you have finished reading a section, you, hopefully, will not be finished thinking. Thus, I invite you to delve into your own thoughts and make your own connections. I merely expect to be a catalyst for responsible study and anticipate that you will allow the Spirit to teach you further.

1
LIVING IN THE LAST DAYS

ONE OF THE BLESSINGS OF LIVING in the last days is that we can study what Christ and His prophets have said about that time and witness the fulfillment of prophecy from conditions and events around us.

The phrase "the last days" conveys many messages to those who consider its meaning. For some, the idea of the last days brings fearful visions of death and destruction. Others envision the last days as the time when faithful individuals will be lifted up into heaven to avoid the tribulations that will befall those left behind. In the large scheme of time, the last days are those within the dispensation of the fulness of times, the last dispensation before the Millennium—the time before the Savior's appearances in glory to usher in the millennial era of peace upon the earth. Thus, those who lived in the nineteenth and twentieth centuries might appropriately be referred to as having lived during the last days. Further, those on the earth today are living in the last days, and those who are born and live on the earth at any time before the Second Coming will live during the last days. The designation of the last days might also refer to the last days of the earth's temporal existence, in which wickedness will be tolerated but come to an end as righteousness is ushered in.

This chapter provides the opportunity to reflect on conditions that have existed and events that have occurred in the past that are an essential part to understanding the last days. In addition, we will consider how current conditions fulfill prophecies regarding the last days, and further chapters will suggest how one might envision the last days that are yet to come.

The Last Days Are Like Childbirth

A study of the last days reveals times of great joy and anticipation, as well as the accompanying challenges. The Apostle Paul likened the last days to a woman who is about to give birth: "For yourselves know perfectly that the day of the Lord . . . cometh upon them, as travail upon a woman with child" (1 Thessalonians 5:2–3).

Let's consider the experience of an expectant mother. She recognizes that something has changed in her life in the weeks following conception; she sees signs that she is indeed expecting a baby. Initially, she is elated with anticipation of a baby coming into the family. She is thrilled to tears to share the news with her husband. However, weeks of morning sickness interrupt this joy. Reality begins to dawn on her husband that his sweetheart is making a great sacrifice to become a mother. They announce to their family and friends that she is expecting. As the months pass, she begins to expand, and it becomes more evident to even the casual observer that a child is about to be born. The expectant mother and her husband count the days until she will give birth. They prepare to receive a child in their home, painting the room next to their bedroom and purchasing a crib, diapers, blankets, clothing, and other necessities. Toward the latter stages of pregnancy, this sweet mother-to-be becomes increasingly uncomfortable. When labor begins, pains accompanying childbirth become sudden and intense, and it seems they are never going to end. Through the discomfort and anxiety, the expectant mother hangs on to the knowledge that a child will soon be born; this will turn out all right! She hears the cry of the baby, and the newborn is placed in her arms. Her husband looks upon mother and child with greater love than he ever dreamed he could experience. She looks up, and her eyes meet her husband's eyes. They have brought a soul into mortality. It is a miracle!

Likewise, the last days are the days, months, years, decades, and even centuries that precede the Second Coming of Jesus Christ. Christ's followers may have received with excitement the initial signs that the time had finally arrived. Similar to parents receiving the joyful announcement that they are expecting a child, angels announced tidings of great joy that we are living in the last dispensation of the gospel before the Savior returns. Indeed, it is a common response on an individual basis to feel an initial excitement in learning of the events and conditions that will occur in connection with the last days and Christ's Second Coming. However, as time passes and reality strikes concerning what it actually means to live in the last days, individuals will need to faithfully deal with the tribulations that require strength of testimony regarding the

Lord's promises. In times of stress, it may seem that the uncomfortable conditions of the last days are never ending, and we might wish that the Lord would simply appear and save us from times of trouble. Returning to Paul's likening the last days to the time preceding childbirth, in addition to pains and tribulations, there are also times of intense joy preceding the Second Coming. Although the mother and father are aware of the painful moments necessary to bring a child into the world, they also have happy moments of anticipation as they prepare for the birth. Similarly, although we know that tribulations will precede the return of Jesus Christ to reign on the earth, we may also participate in the joy of building up Zion in preparation for His appearances. Like parents joyfully announcing that they are expecting a baby and making preparations to have all things ready in their home, we have been commanded to send out announcements of the Lord's coming. As part of the preparation in the last days, the Lord has commanded us to send missionaries into every nation to bear witness of the good news of the Restoration of the gospel. In addition, we organize stakes and strengthen the Saints, build temples and administer sacred ordinances for the living and the dead, and consecrate our efforts to provide for the poor and needy by sending humanitarian aid wherever it is needed. The day will come when the Lord shall look upon our efforts to prepare for His coming and smile with love and appreciation. It will be as if we are caught up in Christ's arms as the righteous are quickened or resurrected to meet Him in the heavens before He descends upon the earth.

Incidentally, often a date for a baby's birth is given based on the best calculation, but alas, the baby may come earlier or later than the due date. It appears that the Savior will appear after what many will consider His due date (see D&C 45:26).

Snapshots of the Last Days

It is not plausible to write in detail every event that has fulfilled prophecies regarding the last days. Instead, one might consider focusing on certain points in time to better understand the conditions that existed as they relate to the ongoing fulfillment of prophecies. If the passage of time in the last days is likened to viewing a video, these points in time are more like snapshot photographs that provide a brief view of life at that moment. The snapshot photographs reveal that prophecies regarding the signs that precede the Second Coming may *begin to be fulfilled* or be in the *process of being fulfilled* without being *completely fulfilled*. This distinction is evident in the Nephite record regarding the signs of the Savior's birth: "And it came to pass that in the commencement of the ninety and second year, behold, the prophecies of the prophets began to be fulfilled more fully; for there began to be greater signs and greater miracles wrought among the people" (3 Nephi 1:4). As you consider the following discussion of moments in time—snapshots of the last days—note that, although all signs of the times may be thought of as "great signs," some may be classified as "greater signs." In each time period discussed, many of the people then living believed the time was at hand for Christ to return because they saw *some of the signs of the times* and seemed to assume that because of those sightings, all of the signs would soon be fulfilled and the Savior would appear.

Like viewing snapshot photographs, we will consider conditions that existed in specific years as they relate to living in the last days. I have chosen the years 1843, 1890, 1918, 1975, 2000, and today (whenever that is), as well as the last days for those in the spirit world. The purpose of this approach is not to be comprehensive of every event leading up to a specific year or of every thought of every person or even most individuals. Rather, by reviewing a few events and statements in a snapshot moment of time, I hope to give an overview of what the last days entail and what they mean to those who have lived and are living in them. Most importantly, hopefully, it will become evident that although the individuals we look at who lived in each of these years died without seeing the Second Coming, they remained sure that, be it in their lifetime or in a future day, all of the prophesied events leading to the Second Coming will be fulfilled and Christ will return to the earth to usher in the promised Millennium. They lived and died in faith, in a "hope for things which are not seen, which are true" (Alma 32:21).

Last Days 1843

Although in hindsight it is obvious that the Second Coming did not occur in 1843 or anytime soon thereafter, it might be instructive to understand the mindset regarding the Second Coming of Christ at that time. Let's suppose you lived in 1843; what evidences and signs of the Second Coming might you have seen fulfilled? It appears that in 1843, many Saints and others not of the Church felt that the Second Coming of Christ was imminent. What might have led them to that belief? To begin, the American culture of the time included many Christians who believed that signs and biblical interpretation pointed to that conclusion. These Christians were referred to as Adventists. One of the Adventists who received considerable press was William Miller. He had intensely studied the Bible. He was rightly convinced through this study that Christ would return to reign physically on the earth after the earth had been cleansed by fire. He was also convinced, though wrongly, that Christ's return was impending. "Miller meticulously calculated that Christ would return near the year 1843, a date he came to through complicated analysis of numbers and symbols drawn mainly from the biblical books of Daniel and Revelation."[3] Many of those who followed Miller's calculations set the date of the Savior's return sometime between March 21, 1843, and March 21, 1844.[4]

Had you lived in that time as a Latter-day Saint, you most likely would have heard of Miller's calculations and added to them the events associated with the recently published prophecies of Enoch (see Moses 7:59–68); in addition, the Prophet Joseph Smith received revelation that clarified and amplified the Savior's Olivet Discourse on the signs of His coming (see D&C 45:16–54; Joseph Smith—Matthew 1:1–40). Long past were the prophesied events of the Apostasy, the establishment of the great and abominable church, the coming forth of the Bible, the Reformation, and the discovery of America and settlement by the Gentiles (see 1 Nephi 13:1–23). The Book of Mormon had come forth, the Church of Jesus Christ was restored, God had called and authorized the Prophet Joseph Smith, and missionaries were going forth to other nations. Significantly, in many of the revelations of the Doctrine and Covenants, the Lord referred to the current era as the "last days" (see D&C 1:4; 20:1; 27:6; 39:11; 52:1; 53:1; 61:14, 17; 63:58; 64:30, 34, 37; 66:2; 84:2; 86:4; 109:23; 112:30; 115:4; 128:17). Most importantly, the prophecy of Malachi that the Lord would send "Elijah the prophet before the coming of the great and dreadful day of the Lord" had been fulfilled (Malachi 4:5). On April 3, 1836, Elijah appeared to the Prophet Joseph Smith and Oliver Cowdery in the Kirtland Temple. Along with Moses and Elias, Elijah committed the keys of this dispensation and explained, "By this ye may know that the great and dreadful day of the Lord is near, even at the doors" (D&C 110:16).

A little over a decade earlier, newspapers reported that those in China had suffered a devastating earthquake. China surely qualified as fulfilling the prophecy that there would be "earthquakes in divers places" (D&C 45:33; JS—M 1:29). There were also other signs and evidences that the Second Coming was near at hand. An article under the heading of "Wars and Rumors of Wars" that ran in the Church's newspaper in Nauvoo, the *Times and Seasons*, gave a clear signal that this sign was being fulfilled:

The civil war in Spain yet continues.

The Mexican and South American Governments have been overwhelmed in wars and revolutions for some time past.

The French and Arabs in Africa are at active war, and have been for some length of time.

Russia and Circassia have been engaged in hostile array during the past season. Much blood has been shed, and from all appearances, the war is likely to continue.

Egypt is making very active preparations of a warlike character, and is threatened by the powers of Europe, who aim to maintain an equilibrium of power in the East.

These, together with the late war between the English and the East Indies, the Canada revolution, and the present war with China, all go to show, that the signs of the times are not of the most peaceful aspect, although we have reason to believe that it is now a time of greater peace and tranquility than will be enjoyed a few years hence. Let us, then, improve the precious time which we now enjoy in preparing for the worst.

From the foregoing accounts, and many other things which have transpired within the last few years, we can all see the fulfillment of a prediction of Moroni, recorded in the Book of Mormon [Mormon 8:29–30]. Speaking of the time when that record should be published to the Gentiles, he says: "It," the record, "shall come in a day when there shall be heard of fires, and tempests, and vapours of smoke in foreign lands; and there shall also be heard of wars and rumors of wars, and earthquakes in divers places." When we see prophecy fulfilling, we are bound to acknowledge that those who uttered it were dictated by the spirit of truth.[5]

Earlier, the Prophet Joseph Smith referred to fulfillment of Joel's prophecy regarding the last days (see Joel 2:30–31; Acts 2:19; 1 Nephi 22:18; D&C 45:40–41). "While in New York I visited the burnt district—the part of the city where it was estimated fifteen millions of property was consumed by fire on the 16th of December, 1835, according to the prediction of the ancient Prophets, that there should be 'fire and vapor of smoke' in the last days."[6]

The Saints were aware that in 1841 the Prophet Joseph Smith commissioned Elder Orson Hyde to travel to Jerusalem, specifically to dedicate the land for the return of the Jewish remnant. Excitement over the forthcoming return of the Jews to the lands of their ancient inheritance pointed to the Savior's appearance on the Mount of Olives. These prophecies and events of the early Church, together with Miller's predictions, might lead one to believe that the Saints anticipated that Christ would return within a very short time. However, the Prophet Joseph Smith corrected any such thoughts. On April 1, 1843, Joseph Smith traveled with Orson Hyde and William Clayton to visit the Saints in Ramus, Illinois, located twenty miles east of Nauvoo. The next day was a Sunday, and the Prophet gave several instructions to the Saints who gathered together. Among those items the Prophet addressed were the speculations regarding the nearness of the Second Coming. "I was once praying very earnestly to know the time of the coming of the Son of Man," he explained, "when I heard a voice repeat the following: Joseph, my son, if thou livest until thou art eighty-five years old, thou shalt see the face of the Son of Man; therefore let this suffice, and trouble me no more on this matter" (D&C 130:14–15). Most instructive is Joseph's commentary regarding his understanding of the meaning of that message. "I was left thus," he continued, "without being able to decide whether this coming referred to the beginning of the millennium or to some previous appearing, or whether I should die and thus see his face" (D&C 130:16). In particular response to the questions of many regarding 1843 or 1844 being the time of Christ's return, the Prophet concluded, "I believe the coming of the Son of Man will not be any sooner than that time [1890, when, had Joseph lived, he would have been eighty-five years old]" (D&C 130:17).

Nearly a year later, the Prophet again addressed concerns regarding the nearness of the Second Coming:

> I have asked of the Lord concerning His coming; and while
> asking the Lord, He gave a sign and said, "In the days of

Noah I set a bow in the heavens as a sign and token that in any year that the bow should be seen the Lord would not come; but there should be seed time and harvest during that year: but whenever you see the bow withdrawn, it shall be a token that there shall be famine, pestilence, and great distress among the nations, and that the coming of the Messiah is not far distant."

But I will take the responsibility upon myself to prophesy in the name of the Lord, that Christ will not come this year, as Father Miller has prophesied, for we have seen the bow; and I also prophesy, in the name of the Lord, that Christ will not come in forty years; and if God ever spoke by my mouth, He will not come in that length of time. Brethren, when you go home, write this down, that it may be remembered.

Jesus Christ never did reveal to any man the precise time that He would come. Go and read the Scriptures, and you cannot find anything that specifies the exact hour He would come; and all that say so are false teachers.[7]

The Prophet Joseph Smith further clarified a few additional events that yet needed to occur before the Savior would return to the earth in glory:

The coming of the Son of Man never will be—never can be till the judgments spoken of for this hour are poured out: which judgments are commenced. . . . Judah must return, Jerusalem must be rebuilt, and the temple, and water come out from under the temple, and the waters of the Dead Sea be healed. It will take some time to rebuild the walls of the city and the temple, &c.; and all this must be done before the Son of Man will make His appearance. There will be wars and rumors of wars, signs in the heavens above and on the earth beneath, the sun turned into darkness and the moon to blood, earthquakes in divers places, the seas heaving beyond their bounds; then will appear one grand sign of the Son of Man in heaven. But what will the world do? They will say it is a planet, a comet, &c. But the Son of Man will come as the sign of the coming of the Son of Man, which will be as the light of the morning cometh out of the east."[8]

During the time of these explanations, the Prophet Joseph Smith also assured the Saints "that God will do nothing but what he will reveal unto his servants the prophets."[9]

Thus it is clear that although prophesied signs were all about in 1843, those who listened to the living Prophet knew they should not become overly concerned with the time of the Second Coming. Indeed, their efforts and emotions could be focused on living righteous lives while continuing to prepare for the future. That is, they could look forward to opportunities to raise families, build homes, plant gardens, gain an education, serve missions, and help build up the kingdom of God on earth.

Last Days 1890

First, consider why I have chosen the year 1890 as the next snapshot in a Latter-day Saint discussion of the last days. Foremost is the fact that the Prophet Joseph Smith speculated that 1890 might be the year the Savior returned in glory to the earth. Clearly, the Prophet believed that the Savior would not return before 1890. Recounting his experience aforementioned, the Prophet Joseph Smith explained:

> I was once praying earnestly upon this subject, and a voice said unto me, "My son, if thou livest until thou art eighty-five years of age, thou shalt see the face of the Son of Man." I was left to draw my own conclusions concerning this; and I took the liberty to conclude that if I did live to that time, He would make His appearance. But I do not say whether He will make His appearance or I shall go where He is. I prophesy in the name of the Lord God, and let it be written—the Son of Man will not come in the clouds of heaven till I am eighty-five years old.[10]

Joseph then read from the Bible, citing both Revelation 14:6–7 and Hosea 6 to point to 1890 as a likely year for the Second Coming. Further, Joseph felt the liberty to surmise, "Were I going to prophesy, I would say the end [of the world] would not come in 1844, 5, or 6, or in forty years. There are those of the rising generation who shall not taste death till Christ comes."[11] As the Prophet Joseph Smith indicated, he took liberty to come to his own conclusions from the scant information he had through revelation in determining a time for the Second Coming. Following his example, during the years that followed the Prophet's death until 1890, other Church leaders and members paid particular attention to that year.

There were other reasons to believe 1890 could be the momentous year of the Savior's return. For example, the Lord revealed to the Prophet Joseph Smith that following a time in which "the Southern States shall be divided against the Northern States" (D&C 87:3), war would be poured out on all nations. During that time, the Saints were to "stand in holy places, and be not moved, until the day of the Lord come; for behold, it cometh quickly, saith the Lord" (D&C 87:8). Nearly thirty years later, the great Civil War broke out in the United States. In addition, the Saints were counseled to gather to stakes in Zion in the Rocky Mountains and take refuge there. Thousands and tens of thousands of those who accepted the Restoration of the gospel left their homes in Great Britain, Scandinavia, Europe, and other countries to make the journey to Salt Lake City. From there, they were sent to colonize areas of the western United States, Mexico, and Canada, in which they established stakes "for a defense, and for a refuge from the storm, and from the wrath when it shall be poured out without mixture on the whole earth" (D&C 115:6).

In addition to these events, the Saints were forced to choose between abiding the laws of the land and practicing plural marriage. The president of the Church of Jesus Christ was Wilford Woodruff. As "the only man on the earth at the present time who [held] the keys of the sealing ordinances," Wilford Woodruff declared his "intention to submit to those laws." He further advised the Saints "to refrain from contracting any marriage forbidden by the law of the land" (Official Declaration 1). The year 1890 must have appeared an ideal time to bring an end to worldly governments and free the Saints to observe all of the laws and practices the Lord had revealed.

One year earlier, in 1889, President Wilford Woodruff gave his view of the nearness of the Second Coming: "Many of these young men and maidens that are here today will, *in my opinion*, if they are faithful, stand in the flesh when Christ comes in the clouds of heaven. These young people from the Sabbath schools and from the Mutual Improvement Associations, will stand in the flesh while the judgments of the Almighty sweep the nations of the earth as with a besom [broom] of destruction, in fulfillment of the revelations of God, and they will be the very people whom God will bless and sustain."[12]

While President Wilford Woodruff and others living at that time might have anticipated the Second Coming in their day and seen the fulfilling of prophecy as evidence that it would be in their day, they were cognizant that they truly did not know the time of the Second Coming. In an article published in the *Deseret Weekly*, October 11, 1890, President Woodruff acknowledged, "I do not think anyone can tell the hour of the coming of the Son of Man. . . . We need not look for the time of that event to be made known." [13]

President Woodruff's counsel to the Saints was, "If the world wants to know what is coming to pass, let them read the Bible, the Book of Mormon, and the Doctrine and Covenants; let them read [the] revelations of St. John. As God lives they will come to pass. Not one of them will fall unfulfilled."[14]

Last Days 1918

Truly, 1918 was a momentous year in the last days. Many events of the past century, and particularly the past thirty years, indicated that Christ's coming must be near at hand. During this year, President Joseph F. Smith passed away and Heber J. Grant became president of the Church. World War I was coming to an end and was arguably the most devastating war in history to that point in time. It involved the people of Europe and had extended across the Atlantic Ocean to pull the United States into the conflict. It appeared that the revelation on wars had possibly been fulfilled, in which Great Britain and other nations needed to call for aid in defending themselves against other nations, after which war was poured out on all nations (D&C 87:3). The collapse of long-standing empires—Russian, German, Austria-Hungarian, and the Ottoman—was imminent. Thus, the fulfillment of the Lord's decree that the inhabitants would feel His chastening hand to make "a full end of all nations" appeared likely in the near future (D&C 87:6). In addition, the turmoil led to missionaries being removed from France, Germany, Switzerland, and Belgium. Could it be that the Lord's servants had given their witness to the world and now the voice of tribulations would be sounded, bringing a full end to wickedness?

It had been nearly a century since God the Father and His Son, Jesus Christ, called Joseph Smith as the Prophet to restore the fulness of the gospel. Great judgments had come "upon the earth, with great desolations by famine, sword, and pestilence" (Joseph Smith—History 1:45). Equally as imposing as World War I, with its toll of thirty-five million casualties—fifteen million dead and twenty million wounded—was the influenza pandemic. Before this scourge ended, an estimated fifty to one hundred million individuals died, with many times more than that surviving, though suffering, and even more fearing what their future might be. Indeed, when President Joseph F. Smith died November 19, 1918, close family and friends held a graveside service rather than a public funeral due to fear of the influenza. Could these events be the fulfillment of the Savior's words that in the generation in which the fulness of the gospel is rejected "they shall see an overflowing scourge; for a desolating sickness shall cover the land. But my disciples shall stand in holy places, and shall not be moved; but among the wicked, men shall lift up their voices and curse God and die" (D&C 45:31–32)?

Before his death, President Joseph F. Smith taught the Saints that "The many eruptions, earthquakes, and tidal waves which have occurred . . . are signs which the Savior declared should foreshadow his second coming. . . . The wise and the prudent will heed the warning and prepare themselves that they be not taken unawares. Not the least of the signs of the times is this, that the gospel is being preached unto the poor, as a witness unto all nations."[15]

Not only had missionary work extended to many nations, but temples were also stretching into foreign lands, across the Pacific Ocean and the Canadian border. Since 1890, in addition to the temples in St. George, Manti, and Logan, the Salt Lake Temple had been completed and dedicated, and a temple in Laie, Hawaii, was nearing completion. Another temple in Cardston, Canada, was announced on June 27, 1913, the anniversary of the martyrdom of the Prophet Joseph Smith and his brother Hyrum.

The signs indicated that the time of the Second Coming was approaching, possibly not even far distant. Nevertheless, there was much that still needed to be accomplished in preparation for the Savior's reign on the earth. Two decades earlier, the First Presidency wrote to the Saints in Turkey, concerned about the seemingly imminent time of the Second Coming. They acknowledged that there were many signs that they lived in the last days, "but there is yet much to do to prepare for that great event. Many of the honest have not yet heard of His great Latter-day work. Zion must be fully established. Jerusalem must be rebuilt by the Jews, the ten tribes must return from the north, the American Indians, who are of the house of Israel must be converted and become workers in His cause. And many more of the different branches of the House of Israel must return to the promised lands and be prepared to meet Him and to receive Him."[16]

Last Days 1975

The events that occurred prior to 1975 pointed to the fact that the earth truly was in its last days. Consider a few of those events. World War I had become known as the Great War and had extended its tentacles beyond Europe and had even laid the groundwork for what would become World War II. Through the Second World War, the Nazi movement had been stopped and the imperial aspirations of the Japanese halted. However, another era had ushered in new world superpowers, the United States and the USSR, with China adding its voice to world events. Missionaries who had been called home during the war had again been sent to share the message of the Restoration of the gospel throughout many nations of the world. The gospel was being sounded in the ears of millions of people—first, through general conference radio broadcasts and then through television broadcasts. Missionaries traveled on airplanes to the far corners of the earth.

In the 1950s, the Church implemented a program to help raise the educational attainment of the American Indians, especially those from tribes in the western United States. Indian students were placed in homes of Latter-day Saints to afford them greater opportunities for education. James B. Allen explained that "from the standpoint of the Navajo students, this was an opportunity to break out of the poverty and ignorance they saw around them and to begin making more positive contributions to their own people."[17] Over the ensuing twenty-five years, many of those who participated appeared to fulfill the prophecy that the "Lamanites shall blossom as the rose" (D&C 49:24). In addition, the Church was growing in Latin American nations, which were associated with the Lamanites. The first stake in South America was organized in Sao Paulo, Brazil, on May 1, 1966.

The decade of the 1960s brought the reality of a nuclear holocaust to the forefront. A confrontation between the United States and the USSR regarding nuclear warhead missiles in Cuba awoke most to the possibilities of the world coming to an end. Bible commentators focused on meanings of symbols in the book of Revelation. Many felt that John had seen modern war machines capable of destroying not only millions and hundreds of millions of the earth's population but even billions.[18] Bomb shelters and food storage were commonplace responses to the signs of the times. Iniquity abounded and continued to grow. The song of the sixties became sexual revolution. Even government agencies touted what was referred to as sexual freedom to the point of supporting killing the unborn in abortions.

Possibly the most important development in fulfilling the signs of the times was the establishment of the state of Israel in Palestine. The vote of the United Nations to establish a Jewish homeland followed the disclosure that at the hands of the Third Reich, thirteen million Jews were exterminated in the Holocaust. Following the War of Independence in 1948–49, the state of Israel included more land than had originally been allocated by the United Nations' mandate but did not encompass the east part of Jerusalem, including the area enclosed by the walls of the Old City. Succeeding wars between Israel and her Arab neighbors in 1967 and again in 1973 brought Jerusalem under Jewish control. Thus, both the Savior's prophecy that the Jews would be scattered and gathered again before His return, as well as that "Jerusalem shall be trodden down of the Gentiles, until the times of the Gentiles be fulfilled" were realized (Luke 21:24). The gathering to Jerusalem foreshadows the period in which the "*times of the Jews* shall begin; that is," wrote Elder Bruce R. McConkie, "the era will commence in which the Jews shall accept the gospel and be blessed spiritually in an abundant way."[19]

On October 5, 1973, a coalition of Arab states, led by Egypt and Syria, launched a surprise attack on Israel on the holiest day in Judaism— Yom Kippur. At the time that President Harold B. Lee spoke in the closing session of general conference on October 7, no one knew to what extent the conflict might escalate. President Lee commented:

> One of the anxious centers right today is over in Israel, where a war is raging. As yet we don't know very much about the extent of it, but it seems that Egypt and Syria are moving into areas of Israel.
>
> We have a number of our BYU students there, and also we have a branch of the Church organized in Jerusalem. We have had anxious parents who have been wondering, watching, waiting. The word has come to us that they are all safe and they are being watched over. You can be sure that we have shepherds of the flock, and we will continue to pray with you that no harm will come to any of them.
>
> There has been turmoil down in Chile, where we have thousands of members of the Church and almost two hundred missionaries. The word comes to us, from one of the presiding authorities who has been here from Santiago, that there has been no loss of life as far as we know. Our people are holding fast, not taking part in the political turmoil, rising above it, as true members of the Church of Jesus Christ are expected to do, giving allegiance to

those who are in command, and not wishing to take sides, but merely to bow their heads and yield obedience to the authority of the government where they are.[20]

President Lee read major portions of the Savior's Olivet Discourse concerning the signs of the Second Coming from the Joseph Smith translation of Matthew 24. He closed by admonishing, "Brothers and sisters, this is the day the Lord is speaking of. You see the signs are here. Be ye therefore ready. The Brethren have told you in this conference how to prepare to be ready."[21]

It was appropriate to see the signs of the times pointing to the nations of the earth gathering against Jerusalem as foretold by the Old Testament prophet Zechariah. The question on many minds was how soon the culminating events leading to the Savior's appearance to the Jewish remnant on the Mount of Olives would occur. It appeared that the events were lined up for an impending fulfillment of the Savior's return. The leaves of the fig tree regarding the Jewish remnant in Jerusalem were beginning to appear. Yet, there was more that needed to occur in preparation for the coming of the Son of Man.

The next general conference, President Spencer W. Kimball, successor to President Lee, who died only a few months after his final conference address, spoke at a regional representatives seminar on Thursday, April 4, 1974. He presented a plan to take the message of the Restoration to all the world. He commented:

> As I read the scripture I think of the numerous nations that are still untouched. I know they have curtains, like iron curtains and bamboo curtains. I know how difficult it is because we have made some efforts. Surely the Lord knew what he was doing when he commanded [that the gospel be taken to the whole earth]. . . . Somehow, brethren, I feel that when we have done all in our power that the Lord will find a way to open doors. That is my faith.
>
> Is any thing too hard for the Lord? . . .
>
> But I can see no good reason why the Lord would open doors that we are not prepared to enter. Why should he break down the Iron Curtain or the Bamboo Curtain or any other curtain if we are still unprepared to enter?
>
> I believe we have men who could help the apostles to open these doors—statesmen, able and trustworthy—but, when we are ready for them.

Today we have 18,600 missionaries. We can send more. Many more![22]

In addition, the first Quorum of Seventy was reorganized in October 1975. The Seventy have a special assignment to "preach the gospel, and to be especial witnesses unto the Gentiles and in all the world" (D&C 107:25). It seemed that the Lord's prophecy that "this Gospel of the Kingdom shall be preached in all the world, for a witness unto all nations" (Joseph Smith—Matthew 1:31) was within reach of being fulfilled! The Savior had foretold that "then shall the end come or the destruction of the wicked" (Joseph Smith—Matthew 1:31).

Yet, the voices of the Lord's servants among the Saints were constant in diffusing the speculative surges that anyone knew when the Savior would return. Addressing the Saints at the October 1972 general conference, President Harold B. Lee noted, "I understand that there is a widely circulated story that I was alleged to have a patriarchal blessing (I don't know whether any of you have heard about that) that had to do with the coming of the Savior and the ten tribes of Israel."[23] After teaching the necessity of receiving authorized statements through approved channels, rather than rumor and gossip, he warned:

> One more matter: There are among us many loose writings predicting the calamities which are about to overtake us. Some of these have been publicized as though they were necessary to wake up the world to the horrors about to overtake us. Many of these are from sources upon which there cannot be unquestioned reliance.
>
> Are you priesthood bearers aware of the fact that we need no such publications to be forewarned, if we were only conversant with what the scriptures have already spoken to us in plainness?
>
> Let me give you the sure word of prophecy on which you should rely for your guide instead of these strange sources which may have great political implications. . . . Brethren, [the scriptures are] the writings with which you should concern yourselves, rather than commentaries that may come from those whose information may not be the most reliable and whose motives may be subject to question.[24]

I am old enough to remember the context of the times of President Lee's counsel to the Church. For example, I recall being informed by a family member about a story shared in the adult Gospel Doctrine class in Sunday School that indicated the Savior was returning very soon. Purportedly, Spencer W. Kimball had a vision or dream of the Savior. The story told was that President Kimball painted a picture of the Savior and gave it to President Lee so he could recognize Christ when he returned. The time of the Second Coming was not fulfilled, but those living in 1975 were living in the last days. Notwithstanding the sensational stories and dreams circulating among Church members, careful study of the scriptures served as a protection against unwarranted fears and expectations. Signs abounded in fulfillment of many prophecies, yet the scriptures were clear that the Lord had revealed more that needed to occur before He would return.

Last Days 2000

Many looked to the year AD 2000 as the year of the Second Coming. Based on the idea that the Savior would return at the opening of the seventh seal of the book of Revelation in the Bible, the year 2000 was a hoped-for landmark in time. Again, it was evident that 2000 was the beginning of a new millennium, but it was not the year of the Second Coming. On the other hand, many events had occurred that prepared the world for the Savior's return. For example, throughout the previous decade, many of the nations that had been closed to missionaries behind the Iron Curtain opened their doors to the gospel. Senior couples, young men, and young women were opening letters from the president of the Church that stated they had been called to serve in Ukraine, Russia, Poland, Hungary, Lithuania, and more. By December 1989, the loosening of the Communist party's stranglehold on Eastern Europe was the Lord's Christmas present to the world. In the early 1990s, the world changed dramatically with the independence of all fifteen republics in the Soviet Union. This change also caused a reevaluation of earlier ideas involving the United States and the USSR leading two great coalitions of good versus evil in a great latter-day showdown at Armageddon.[25]

As dramatic as the events in Eastern Europe had been, a decade earlier the doors for missionary work had effectually been opened to the African nations. On June 8, 1978, the First Presidency of the Church announced that President Spencer W. Kimball, in company with his counselors and members of the Quorum of the Twelve Apostles, had received a revelation. After considerable supplication, they announced that God "has heard our prayers, and by revelation has confirmed that the long-promised day has come when every faithful, worthy man in the Church may receive the priesthood" (Official Declaration 2). Native Africans could now administer all of the ordinances of The Church of Jesus Christ of Latter-day Saints and preside with priesthood authority and keys. By 1997 there were more than 100,000 members of the Church on the African continent.

Africa also became the center of attention for another reason—famine. As a result of war, government policies, and drought, more than 400,000 people died in northern Ethiopia. Church members in the United States and Canada joined in a special fast to raise relief funds to send to victims. The fast, the six million dollars raised, and the commodities sent to Ethiopia and other areas of need in the world brought two important moments to the forefront. First, the Lord's reference to famine in the last days was not an idle comment (Joseph Smith—Matthew 1:29). Second, the efforts to reach out to the needy began the Church's major efforts in providing humanitarian aid. By the year 2000, members of the Church had seen that, in comparison to any previous dispensation or previous generation, those living in the last days would have greater opportunities to help the poor and needy as the prophecies of the Savior concerning wars, famines, pestilences, and earthquakes were fulfilled.

Focus again came to the Middle East when in 1989 the Brigham Young University Jerusalem Center for Near Eastern Studies was dedicated and unfounded rumors began that the expansive building of student dormitories and classrooms would become a temple someday in the near future. In 1996, the Church reached a milestone when more members lived outside the United States than in it. A temple in Hong Kong gave China its first temple when Hong Kong became part of that nation in 1997. At the end of 2000, there were more than one hundred temples in thirty countries, with thirty-four being dedicated that year alone. More than 60,000 missionaries were serving in approximately eighty-five nations. During his administration, President Ezra Taft Benson called on the Saints to return to studying the Book of Mormon. In the year 2000, the one hundred millionth copy of the Book of Mormon since 1830 was published, and the Book of Mormon had been translated into one hundred languages. As special witnesses of Christ, the First Presidency and the Quorum of the Twelve sent their testimonies to all of the world in a document entitled, "The Living Christ." Again, the long-anticipated return of the Savior had not occurred, but the signs were all about that the prophecies were and soon could be fulfilled.

The Last Days for Those in the Spirit World

The Second Coming is a major event on both sides of the veil. In context of his discourse on the destruction of Jerusalem in AD 70 and the signs of the Second Coming, the Savior referred to promises made of the Resurrection and of the restoration of Israel. It became evident that those who had lived and were to live on the earth would spend considerable time in the spirit world awaiting the Second Coming. Recognizing that His disciples had "looked upon the long absence of [their] spirits from [their] bodies to be a bondage," Christ explained "how the day of redemption shall come" (D&C 45:17). There are many in the spirit world who have "departed the mortal life, firm in the hope of a glorious resurrection, through the grace of God the Father and his Only Begotten Son, Jesus Christ" (D&C 138:14). Further, many more postmortal spirits have been "taught faith in God, repentance from sin, vicarious baptism for the remission of sins, the gift of the Holy Ghost by the laying on of hands, and all other principles of the gospel" (D&C 138:33–34).

The glorious day of resurrection for many of those in the spirit world is directly related to the signs of Christ's Second Coming. Many in the spirit world are aware that "they who have slept in their graves shall come forth, for their graves shall be opened; and they also shall be caught up to meet him in the midst of the pillar of heaven" (D&C 88:97). On the other hand, there are many spirits "who received not the gospel of Christ, neither the testimony of Jesus . . . who shall not be redeemed from the devil until the last resurrection" (D&C 76:82, 85).

The Prophet Joseph Smith offered some insight as to the importance of postmortal spirits knowing the signs of the times and preparing for Christ's Second Coming. In 1839, while instructing the Twelve prior to their mission to Great Britain, the Prophet declared, "I testify of these things, and that the coming of the Son of Man is nigh, even at your doors. If our souls and our bodies are not looking forth for the coming of the Son of Man; and *after we are dead*, if we are not looking forth, we shall be among those who are calling for the rocks to fall upon them."[26]

Joseph continued to teach that the mission of Elijah must have influence in turning the hearts of the children to the fathers and the hearts of the fathers to the children, "living or dead, to prepare them for the coming of the Son of Man."[27] President Joseph F. Smith testified, "I beheld that the faithful elders of this dispensation, when they depart from mortal life, continue their labors in the preaching of the gospel of repentance and redemption, through the sacrifice of the Only Begotten Son of God, among those who are in darkness and under the bondage of sin in the great world of the spirits of the dead" (D&C 138:57). Thus, the work of preparing people for the Second Coming of Christ through the preaching of the gospel occurs on both sides of the veil.

Further, the Prophet Joseph Smith taught that "the spirits of the just . . . are not far from us, and know and understand our thoughts, feelings, and motions."[28] Along with other events in mortality, it appears likely that the signs of the last days are momentous events for those in the spirit world in signaling that a day of major judgment is approaching. Those who are prepared will come forth in the resurrection of the just to enjoy the blessings of the Millennium. On the other hand, those who are not prepared will see a great change in the spirit world as many of the righteous leave that sphere in order to progress. The desolation of abomination will be fulfilled by the wrath of God being poured out not only upon the wicked in mortality but also upon those in the spirit world. The Lord referred to missionary work in mortality and in the spirit world as a means to prepare individuals "that their souls may escape the wrath of God, the desolation of abomination which awaits the wicked, both in this world and in the world to come" (D&C 88:85).

President Brigham Young shared that after the martyrdom, the Prophet Joseph Smith visited him on several occasions. In those visits, among other items, Joseph explained that he was engaged in a great work on the other side, preparing the people there for the Second Coming of the Lord. "Father Smith and Carlos and brother Partridge, yes, and every other good Saint, are just as busy in the spirit world as you and I are here," Brigham explained. "They can see us, but we cannot see them unless our eyes were opened. What are they doing there? They are preaching, preaching all the time, and preparing the way for us to hasten our work in building temples here and elsewhere, and to go back to Jackson County and build the great temple of the Lord. They are hurrying to get ready by the time we are ready, and we are all hurrying to get ready by the time our Elder Brother is ready."[29]

President Wilford Woodruff also testified:

> Joseph Smith visited me a great deal after his death, and taught me many important principles. . . . I saw him at the door of the temple in heaven. He came to me and spoke to me. He said he could not stop to talk with me because he was in a hurry. The next man I met was Father Smith; he could not talk with me because he was in a hurry. I met a half a dozen brethren who had held high positions on earth, and none of them could stop to talk with me because they were in a hurry. I was much astonished. By and by I saw the Prophet again and got the privilege of asking him a question.
>
> "Now," said I, "I want to know why you are in a hurry. I have been in a hurry all my life; but I expected my hurry would be over when I got into the kingdom of heaven, if I ever did."
>
> Joseph said: "I will tell you, Brother Woodruff. Every dispensation that has had the priesthood on the earth and has gone into the celestial kingdom has had a certain amount of work to do to prepare to go to the earth with the Savior when he goes to reign on the earth. We have not. We are the last dispensation, and so much work has to be done, and we need to be in a hurry in order to accomplish it."[30]

Thus, apparently, many of those in the spirit world are well aware of the era of the last days and sense a need to be prepared. Millions were members of the Church of Jesus Christ in mortality and may have anticipated Christ's return before they died. Perhaps, now it might be said that they look forward to the Second Coming with even greater anticipation than do those in mortality. Before the Savior makes His appearances with the Saints in the clouds of heaven, those in the spirit world will have been prepared for their duties that will follow in the millennial work.

Last Days Today

Reflecting on the events of the past centuries—which fulfill the Savior's description of the last days—helps us gain a better perspective of the prophecies associated with that time than in any previous generation. The Twelve Apostles of the meridian of time had hoped that Christ would return in their lifetime. The Savior warned them that there would be "false Christs, and false prophets, [who] shall show great signs and wonders, insomuch, that, if possible, they shall deceive the very elect, who are the elect according to the covenant" (Joseph Smith—Matthew 1:22). "Behold, I speak these things unto you for the elect's sake; and you also shall hear of wars, and rumors of wars; see that ye be not troubled, for all I have told you must come to pass; but the end is not yet" (Joseph Smith—Matthew 1:23).

Thus, it appears that the wars and perplexities of nations are indications of the last days but not final signs of the end of times. We have heard and will continue to hear of nations at war and citizens of nations who have been treated as slaves rising up against their masters, disciplined for war (see D&C 87:4). Likewise, many, if not all of the signs that have been fulfilled will continue to be fulfilled over and over. If there is any lesson to be learned from the snapshots of time we have considered, it is that living in the last days has no specified time period. The last days and signs of them will continue until the Savior returns in glory.

Every reader should write what it is like to live in the last days of today. Indeed, such reflection will bring added insight into clearer understanding and fulfillment of the signs of the times. Specific conditions of the last days will change with each new development in the latest news headline and the latest progress of The Church of Jesus Christ of Latter-day Saints. I believe latter-day prophets and apostles will continue to teach the scriptural warnings regarding the last days as has occurred in the past. Most likely, they and the Saints will continue to make application of prophecies regarding the conditions of the last days to the conditions surrounding them. One lesson we can learn from the past is that we should not confuse proper interpretation of prophecy with application of prophecy. For example, application of modern government leaders to the beasts mentioned in the book of Revelation may be relevant. However, that does not indicate that any particular individual is definitely the one meant to be the interpretation of the prophecy. Each time a new threat to the state of Israel arises in the Middle East, individuals begin to declare that the stage is now set for the great battle of Gog and Magog. We can see how the prophecies may be fulfilled given current conditions. Nevertheless, wisdom dictates that we recognize the role of prophetic application and not confuse it with ultimate prophetic fulfillment.

For a glimpse of the future, the following chapters will discuss specific prophesied conditions of the last days. As to the nearness of the Second

Coming within the context of the last days, it is important to note that nearly all of the revelations referring to this time indicate that the time of the Savior's return is at the very doors, waiting to enter.

A humorous anecdote illustrates the relative nature of time and the use of revelatory phrases referring to the Second Coming, such as, "I come quickly" (D&C 33:18) and "the great and dreadful day of the Lord is near, even at the doors" (D&C 110:16). The story goes like this: A man has a conversation with God in which he asks if the relation of time in heaven is really one day to God and one thousand years to mortal man on earth. After God answered in the affirmative, the man asked Him if that ratio was also true of other things, to which God again answered in the affirmative, that approximately three hundred and sixty-five thousand to one was a common ratio. Recognizably pleased, the man asked, "Could I have just ten heavenly dollars?" God responded, "Of course, give me just a minute and I will be right with you."

The Lord revealed, "It is called today until the coming of the Son of Man" (D&C 64:23). Thus, whenever the Savior may return, He will return today. In addition, the reference to the Savior coming quickly does not indicate the nearness of His Second Coming. Rather, as illustrated in the parable of the ten virgins, there will not be time to prepare after the Savior comes. Such preparation must have been made previous to His appearances.

2
SIGNS OF THE LAST DAYS

WE ARE UNDER DIVINE ADMONITION to watch for the signal events of the last days and prepare for them, whether they are glorious in nature or calamitous. Some events and the preparation needed to bring them to pass may be joyful, such as building, dedicating, and receiving ordinances in temples and preaching the gospel to every nation. On the other hand, additional events may bring sorrow and require preparation for challenging times, such as wars, earthquakes, and famines. Regarding the events of the last days, the Lord revealed, "And it shall come to pass that he that feareth me shall be looking forth for the great day of the Lord to come, even for the signs of the coming of the Son of Man" (D&C 45:39). Further, the Lord cautioned that "the coming of the Lord draweth nigh, and it overtaketh the world as a thief in the night—therefore, gird up your loins, that you may be the children of light, and that day shall not overtake you as a thief" (D&C 106:4–5).

The main purposes for knowing the signs of the times are to encourage us to prepare for the coming of the Savior and to teach us how to prepare. Rather than rousing despairingly paralyzing fear, recognizing the fulfillment of the prophecies regarding the last days should inspire hope and encouragement that wickedness will soon end and be replaced by the millennial era of peace and righteousness. Occasionally, individuals worry themselves about knowing the exact time of the Second Coming. In reality, they simply wish to know how much longer they have to either repent or endure. Prudently, the Lord has kept the time of His return unknown. Indeed, He has openly indicated that "the hour and the day no man knoweth, neither the angels in heaven, nor shall they know until he comes" (D&C 49:7). However, He has also indicated that the wise will know the signs of His coming and make the necessary preparations to meet the challenges of wars, famines, pestilences, earthquakes, and wickedness. Perhaps most importantly, those living in the last days should see in the signs indications that there will be an increasing need to reach out to others who are suffering from the physical and social conditions of the era.

There are many appropriate approaches to understanding the last days. Some have undertaken to make lists of signs and provide a type of checklist to be marked off. Once all of the boxes have been checked, the Second Coming must be imminent. Admittedly, there are some signs that will occur immediately before the Savior returns; however, the length of time that various prophesied events will occur or the time between one of the events to another is not clear. Thus, the checklist method may not provide the very information that is attributed to it. Such declaration is by no means admonition to be ignorant regarding the signs. Rather, one needs to be aware of them, ponder the Savior's purposes for revealing such events, and see within the work of the Restoration directions to prepare for and fulfill the Savior's words.

The experiences of the last days may be as varied as each individual is different from another. In a grand scale, consider the difference between those who hear of wars and rumors of wars in foreign lands and those who intimately experience the devastation of war in their own land. Further, as has already been experienced in recent natural disasters, there is a grand separation between those who are near the epicenter of an earthquake on land and those who live near the ocean. In the latter situation, the earthquakes are followed by tsunami waves that may take more lives and destroy more homes and businesses than the initial earthquake. Furthermore, those who are far from the epicenter of the earthquake may send aid to the victims or may be able to travel to that area to be personally involved in humanitarian efforts. It becomes clear that painting one general picture of the last days that describes every individual's experiences is not a very realistic proposition.

What follows is like an artist's attempt to paint an intricate panoramic work of the last days on a canvas. In this case, the colors will be in the form of words, often word pictures, divided into three hues to distinguish prominent themes and allow the viewer to gaze upon the result hour after hour in contemplation. Hopefully, each viewing will reveal new insights and give new inspiration to better understand the truth being portrayed in the details of each element of the painting.

Is That True? What Sources and Interpretations Can Be Trusted?

Many articles, books, firesides, lessons, and talks have been written or given concerning the last days. We must decide which sources we accept as authoritative on the subject, and we must determine how to interpret those sources. As individuals determine which sources they trust, they also decide the degree of error they are willing to accept. Some accept everything that has been written or even remembered in connection to the Second Coming.

For example, I vividly recall my personal experience as a young high school seminary student in the late 1960s and early 1970s. My teacher followed the flow of thinking in that era and based his teachings regarding the last days on a widely held book that included spurious information attributed to the Prophet Joseph Smith. The author of that book was a popular fireside and youth conference speaker. My teacher created an outline on the chalkboard from the material in that book. As students, we were all expected to copy the outline from the board and memorize it for an exam. I do not lay any ill intent on his part to deceive us concerning the signs of the times; rather, I think it's sad that he was so willing to accept and teach from questionable sources in an effort to be the most recent word on the last days instead of focusing on what the apostles and prophets taught, no matter how long ago it may have been. The outlines from the book were merely fanciful thinking that has since been proven faulty in its conclusion.

Others have determined to base their books and articles concerning the last days on compilations of excerpts from talks by General Authorities. This approach introduces the reader to the best thinking of General Authorities throughout the last two hundred years. It should be noted that the General Authorities often likened the prophecies in the scriptures to their own day. Thus, any similarity of events from prophesied conditions in the scriptures and the General Authorities' current situations were determined to be fulfillment of the prophecies or at least insight into how the prophecies might be fulfilled. Care should be taken in differentiating between likening last-day prophecies and doctrinal interpretation. There is a distinction between best thinking and divine revelation.

The interpretation of the scriptures and prophetic utterances has given us a wide array of source material regarding the last days. The first determination the reader should make in interpreting prophecy is whether the passage of scripture or the prophetic statement actually addresses conditions of the last days or is being stretched or likened to the last days. For example, if we lived in the generation of the Savior's mortal ministry, how would we know beforehand which scriptural passages foretold of the Savior's mortal life and which addressed His Second Coming?

Consider Zechariah's words to the daughters of Zion and Jerusalem, that their King will come "riding upon an ass, and upon a colt the foal of an ass" (Zechariah 9:9). Before Jesus Christ came riding into Jerusalem on the last Sunday of His life, exactly as Zechariah described, one might not have been sure of which coming these words referred to. Further, how can we know which prophecies will have more than one fulfillment? Is it possible that when the Savior appears on the Mount of Olives to the Jewish remnant, He will afterward again enter the city in fulfilling detail of Zechariah's prophecy? Furthermore, will all of the prophecies find dual fulfillment?

Elder Bruce R. McConkie wrote from the perspective that many of the Old Testament prophecies concerning destruction of ancient wicked kingdoms, societies, and cities were types for the destruction of the wicked in the last days.[31] How do we determine how much to focus on whether Isaiah's prophecies concerning the destruction of Assyria and Babylon are equally specific prophecy for the last days? For instance, will Assyria or the modern peoples that inhabit the land of ancient Assyria again be "the rod of mine anger" to chasten Jerusalem before they are destroyed themselves (Isaiah 10:5)? Will that chastening be followed by the rise of a modern Babylon that brings hosts to battle against Jerusalem and lays it to waste before Babylon's own destruction (see Isaiah 13)?

One can readily discern that there might be wisdom in considering those prophecies that have high reliability of last-day fulfillment and take secondary consideration for other prophecies and dual fulfillments that may refer to the last days as well as earlier time periods.

An approach to solving the uncertainty of which prophecies refer to the last days or which are dual in fulfillment is to build a foundation upon revelation that has been given, clarified, or referred to in latter-day scripture or the revelations and teachings of latter-day presidents of the Church. Prophets may both direct the people of their day and foretell of events for a future time. However, sensibly, the ministry of each prophet will center in the events that most affect their own day. The head of each dispensation of the gospel will be given the mission for that dispensation and vision of how that mission fits into God's overall plan of all dispensations. Consequently, the Prophet Joseph Smith and those prophets who have held the keys of the kingdom after him will address more of the last days than those prophets who came before them.

Prophetic Discourses on the Last Days
The Signs of the Second Coming Shown to Enoch
(Moses 7:59–68)

The scriptures have many allusions to the Second Coming and the signs that will precede it, but there have been only a handful of scriptural discourses specifically intended to instruct concerning the signs of the Savior's return to earth. It may be most helpful to consider the first of those discourses that have been preserved as a basic outline before adding additional insights to the story.

Although Adam must have addressed the Second Coming when, "being full of the Holy Ghost, [he] predicted whatsoever should befall his posterity unto the latest generation" (D&C 107:56), Enoch's is the earliest record made known to us today concerning the signs of the Second Coming. There are three clear themes in Enoch's vision concerning the last days: (1) wickedness, (2) tribulations, and (3) restored truth and righteousness. Clearly, the prophet Enoch knew of the coming of the Son of Man in the flesh and that God's plan included a time for the earth to rest from wickedness. He was not as clear on the timing of these events or if there was a correlation between them. The Lord showed him in a sweeping panoramic vision the future of the earth and its inhabitants.

He saw in each dispensational vision that the prophets sought to turn the tide of wickedness and sorrowed over iniquity and its resultant destruction of the people (see Moses 7:41–53). Enoch asked the Lord, "When the Son of Man cometh in the flesh, shall the earth rest? I pray thee, show me these things" (Moses 7:54). To his sorrow, he learned that the time for earth's rest was not during the Savior's mortal ministry. Rather, he saw that Christ would be "lifted up on the cross" and that the creations of God would mourn (Moses 7:55–56). Further, the Son of God would not return after men had learned to live in peace and look forward to a Millennium in which Christ would reign on the earth. Contrarily, "the Lord said unto Enoch: As I live, even so will I come in the last days, in the days of wickedness and vengeance" (Moses 7:60).

Thus, we see that from early dispensations the Lord revealed that wicked conditions would exist in the last days. Later, the Savior referred to the last days as an era when "iniquity shall abound" (D&C 45:27). But these wicked conditions are not unique to the last days. Even in Enoch's day, he saw that "the power of Satan was upon all the face of the earth . . . and he beheld Satan; and he had a great chain in his hand, and it veiled the whole face of the earth with darkness; and he looked up and laughed, and his angels rejoiced" (Moses 7:24, 26). Similarly, the Lord showed Enoch that in the last days "the heavens shall be darkened, and a veil of darkness shall cover the earth; and the heavens shall shake, and also the earth; and great tribulations shall be among the children of men" (Moses 7:61).

But the Lord promised to counteract the prophesied wickedness. He explained to Enoch, "Righteousness will I send down out of heaven; and truth will I send forth from out of the earth, to bear testimony of mine Only Begotten . . . and righteousness and truth will I cause to sweep the earth as with a flood" (Moses 7:62). Among the many events appropriately seen as fulfillments of the promise to send righteousness from heaven is the young Joseph Smith's vision of the Father and the Son in 1820. Added to that First Vision has been a flood of visions, angelic visitations, and revelations, all pieces in the Restoration of the gospel in the last days. One of the greatest was the coming forth of the gold plates from the Hill Cumorah, which realized the vision of truth coming from out of the earth.

Wickedness has endured on the earth since the days of Adam, but the Lord specifically promised Enoch that He would restore truth and righteousness to the earth in the last days. During the days of Enoch, the righteous people living in the city of Zion were "taken up into heaven" (Moses 7:21). Enoch was shown that he and the citizens of Zion would return to the earth in the last days as an era of millennial rest is ushered in. "But before that day he saw great tribulations among the wicked; and he also saw the sea, that it was troubled, and men's hearts failing them, looking forth with fear for the judgments of the Almighty God, which should come upon the wicked" (Moses 7:66).

Thus, in review, the general synopsis of the last days, as shown to Enoch, emphasized a time of wickedness, tribulation, and truth being restored. It is noteworthy that the Lord used general descriptions to illustrate the time when He would return to the earth in glory but that He did not choose to reveal greater detail for those who lived in Enoch's day. Nevertheless, for those who live in the last days, the Lord has revealed more concerning these three themes. In the Spirit of simplicity and clarity, each of these themes will be examined in chapters that follow, although some interweaving may be necessary, as they are all part of the same story of the last days.

The Savior's Olivet Discourse
(Matthew 24; Mark 13; Luke 21; D&C 45; Joseph Smith—Matthew)

The clearest discourse on the Second Coming came from the Savior's own lips. On Tuesday of the last week of His mortal life, Jesus Christ sat upon the hillside known as the Mount of Olives, to the east of Jerusalem, where He taught His disciples. The disciples had inquired concerning His declaration that not one stone of the temple mount buildings would be left upon another but that they would all be thrown down. The disciples asked, "Tell us when shall these things be which thou hast said concerning the destruction of the temple, and the Jews; and what is the sign of thy coming, and of the end of the world, or the destruction of the wicked, which is the end of the world" (Joseph Smith—Matthew 1:4)? The Savior's answer to those questions is recorded in Matthew 24, Mark 13, and Luke 21.

On March 7, 1831, the Savior revealed to the Prophet Joseph Smith greater clarity concerning His discussion with His meridian-day disciples (see D&C 45:16–53). During the previous nine months, the Prophet Joseph Smith had been engaged in an inspired translation of the Bible, beginning with the Old Testament book of Genesis. The Lord had informed him that "it shall not be given unto you to know any further concerning this chapter [Matthew 24], until the New Testament be translated, and in it all these things shall be made known" (D&C 45:60). The Lord further directed the Prophet, "Ye may now translate it [the New Testament], that ye may be prepared for the things to come" (D&C 45:61). In time, Matthew 24 was clarified with prophetic inspiration and published to the world as Joseph Smith—Matthew in the Pearl of Great Price. The text of the Joseph Smith translation of Mark 13 is the same as in Joseph Smith—Matthew. The Joseph Smith Translation account in Luke 21 retains an abbreviated but insightful discussion of that same day on the Mount of Olives.

Because these records from that one discourse on the Mount of Olives inform us of the Savior's teachings regarding the signs of His coming, they all appropriately carry the title of the "Olivet Discourse," both individually and collectively. Appropriately, they form the foundation upon which we can build our understanding of all other visions and revelations regarding the last days.

Following a discussion of the destruction of Jerusalem and the signs of the times for that generation, the Savior foretold the Apostasy that would ensue and take hold of the world until the last days. Christ warned that during that time of apostasy, false Christs and false prophets would arise and deceive those of the covenant. In addition, that era of apostasy would be one of wars and rumors of wars. However, the Savior emphatically declared, "But the end is not yet" (Joseph Smith—Matthew 1:23). Further, He warned that His return would not be in the desert or in secret chambers, "for as the light of the morning cometh out of the east, and shineth even unto the west, and covereth the whole earth, so shall the coming of the Son of Man be" (Joseph Smith—Matthew 1:26).

The Savior foretold that during the era of the Great Apostasy, following the destruction of Jerusalem in AD 70, a remnant of the Jewish nation would be "scattered among all nations; but they shall be gathered again; but they shall remain until the times of the Gentiles be fulfilled" (D&C 45:24–25). The gathering of the Jewish remnant to Jerusalem and surrounding areas is one of the most easily identifiable signs of the times. It signals the fulfillment of the time of the Gentiles, the present era in which we live; that is, today is a time of taking the message of the Restoration to non-Jewish peoples. The Savior promised a day, though, in which the focus of taking the message of the Restoration to the Gentile nations would shift to also include bearing witness to the Jewish remnant once again.

The Savior explained to His disciples, as He stood before them in the flesh on Olivet, that the era of the times of the Gentiles would be similar to the era of the Great Apostasy. Specifically, "in that day shall be heard of wars and rumors of wars, and the whole earth shall be in commotion" (D&C 45:26; Joseph Smith—Matthew 1:28). Further, the mortal Christ foretold of "famines, and pestilences, and earthquakes, in divers places" (Joseph Smith—Matthew 1:29). The results of the great commotion of the last days will be that "men's hearts shall fail them, and they shall say that Christ delayeth his coming until the end of the earth" (D&C 45:26).

The Savior's explanations to His disciples of the signs of His return follow the same three main themes we discussed previously, which are found in Enoch's vision of the last days. The Savior foreordained the restoration of the fulness of the gospel to occur during the era of the times of the Gentiles. Sadly, although the light of the fulness of the gospel will break forth among the Gentiles, the Savior explained that they will not receive it, "and they turn their hearts from me because of the precepts of men" (D&C 45:29).

Thus, similar to Enoch's revelation and a repeat of the Apostasy in the meridian of time, iniquity is a central theme in the last days. Indeed, the Lord referred to the last days as an era in which "because iniquity shall abound, the love of men shall wax cold" (Joseph Smith—Matthew 1:30). Therefore, Christ's servants will fulfill His commission that the "Gospel of the Kingdom shall be preached in all the world, for a witness unto all nations" (Joseph Smith—Matthew 1:31). They will reject this witness because of iniquity and will bring upon themselves their own destruction. Ultimately, the desolation of abomination that took place in the destruction of Jerusalem anciently will occur again in the latter days. (For further discussion of the latter-day destruction of Jerusalem, see the chapter on Christ's appearance to the Jewish remnant gathered at Jerusalem.)

The Lord further explained to His meridian-day disciples that in the midst of the latter-day wickedness, "my disciples shall stand in holy places, and shall not be moved; but among the wicked, men shall lift up their voices and curse God and die" (D&C 45:32). Thus, presumably, the Saints will be aware of the signs of the times and will have prepared spiritually to avoid the stress that accompanies an unsure future in the midst of tribulations. Knowledge of scriptural warnings, teachings of latter-day prophets, and instructions for building holy places of Zion will enable the Saints to face the future with confidence and a surety that the Lord's hand will sustain His people.

The Savior explained that the final signs to precede His coming in glory will be signs in the heavens: "The sun shall be darkened, and the moon shall not give her light, and the stars shall fall from heaven, and the powers of heaven shall be shaken. . . . then shall appear the sign of the Son of Man in heaven. . . . and they shall see the Son of Man coming in the clouds of heaven, with power and great glory" (Joseph Smith— Matthew 1:33, 36). Thus, the Savior answered the disciples' question "concerning the signs of my coming, in the day when I shall come in my glory in the clouds of heaven" (D&C 45:16).

In His Olivet Discourse, the Savior gave signs regarding His appearance to the world. However, He also indicated that before "all the tribes of the earth" will "see the Son of Man coming in the clouds of heaven, with power and great glory" (Joseph Smith—Matthew 1:36), "the saints that have slept shall come forth to meet me in the cloud" (D&C 45:45); in addition, near the time that the wicked will be destroyed, Christ will appear to the Jewish remnant on the Mount of Olives (D&C 45:45–53). The Messiah's appearance to the Jews and its attendant events is a story that requires a separate discussion of its own and is examined in a subsequent chapter.

The Fig Tree Puts Forth Its Leaves: Prophetic Warnings

The Savior likened the signs of His coming to the sign of a fig tree's tender leaves that indicate the season is about to change to summer (see D&C 45:36–38; Joseph Smith—Matthew 1:38–39). "So likewise, mine elect, when they shall see these things, they shall know that he is near, even at the doors," the Lord declared; "but of that day, and hour, no one knoweth; no, not the angels of God in heaven, but my Father only" (Joseph Smith—Matthew 1:39–40). Recording the same discourse, the gospel of Mark states that no man or angels would know the day or the hour, "neither the Son" but only the Father (Mark 13:32). The JST rendering of this text deletes the words "neither the Son," suggesting that the Father *and* Christ know the time of Christ's return. That no man or angel was to know the hour and the day of His return, "nor shall they know until he comes," was reaffirmed in a revelation given in March 1831 (see D&C 49:7).

The Lord has commanded latter-day prophets and apostles to declare that we are living in the last days. Occasionally, unfaithful or uninformed individuals accuse latter-day prophets of telling the people that the Second Coming will occur in their lifetime. Admittedly, prophets and apostles often speak and have spoken on the signs of the last days, pointing out their fulfillments; however, as servants of the Lord, they are simply fulfilling their responsibility to teach the people to be prepared for the Second Coming because it *might* come in their lifetime. What a position to be in! The Lord has not revealed the day of His coming but has given signs of the season of His coming. Those signs have already begun to appear. It behooves the prophets and all the Saints to always be prepared for the Second Coming because it could occur in their lifetime.

Following the recitation of the parable of the fig tree, the Savior likened the last days to the days before the great flood (Joseph Smith—Matthew 1:41–43). No one knew which day the prophesied flood would come to take them away. Then again, after one hundred twenty years of warning the people to repent and preparing for the flood, Noah and his family knew to enter the ark seven days before "the waters of the flood were upon the earth" (Genesis 7:10). Significantly, they did not enter the ark and wait a decade, a year, or even a month. In harmony with the Lord's command to Noah a week before the flood, "Come thou and all thy house into the ark" (Genesis 7:1), the Lord will reveal to His latter-day prophets when the time of His coming is imminent, although His prophets will not know the day or the hour. During April General Conference 1843, the Prophet Joseph Smith assured the Saints at Nauvoo that when the time arrived for the Savior to appear, if not one single person knew, it "would be in flat contradiction with other scripture. For the prophet says that God will do nothing but what he will reveal unto his servants the prophets. Consequently, if it is not made known to the prophets, it will not come to pass."[33]

3
INIQUITY OF THE LAST DAYS

I WOULD VENTURE A GUESS that most offhand remarks about the last days deal with the burning of the wicked. Thus, it should not surprise us that wickedness is a prominent hue on the canvas of the last days and the first theme of the last days that we will discuss. When His disciples inquired about the conditions on earth in the last days, the mortal Christ simply answered, "Because iniquity shall abound, the love of men shall wax cold" (Joseph Smith—Matthew 1:30; see also D&C 45:27).

The foundation for this wickedness is twofold. One measurement for the depth and width of wickedness is individual choices of evil rather than good. The second is a joint effort of individuals in organizations to promote their evil designs. Both come at the cost of rejecting the Spirit of God or the Light of Christ.

First, consider the wickedness in the last days as the prophets have described it. The visions given to prophetic eyes allow us to better understand what is happening, even as we experience it. The Apostle Paul wrote such a lengthy description that it requires reading and slowly rereading just to begin to grasp his words. Imagine painting scenes on our canvas of the last days for each of these descriptions:

"This know also, that in the last days perilous times shall come. For men shall be lovers of their own selves, covetous, boasters, proud, blasphemers, disobedient to parents, unthankful, unholy, without natural affection, trucebreakers, false accusers, incontinent, fierce, despisers of those that are good, traitors, heady, highminded, lovers of pleasures more than lovers of God; having a form of godliness, but denying the power thereof: from such turn away" (2 Timothy 3:1–5).

In October 2001, President Gordon B. Hinckley referred to Paul's warnings and gave prophetic insight into those warnings. He said, "We see today all of these evils, more commonly and generally, than they have ever been seen before. . . . We live in a season when fierce men do terrible and despicable things. We live in a season of war. We live in a season of arrogance. We live in a season of wickedness, pornography, immorality. All of the sins of Sodom and Gomorrah haunt our society. Our young people have never faced a greater challenge. We have never seen more clearly the lecherous face of evil."[34] Thus, the realities of Paul's prophetic description are not unfamiliar to those living in the last days. Rather, Paul's words are lenses that provide clear interpretation for what we experience as well as what we hear reported from other eye- and ear-witnesses.

Sadly, as the Savior explained, when iniquity abounds, the love of men waxes cold, or when wickedness flourishes, prospers, multiplies, and flows across the face of the earth, the flame that should soften each heart, engendering compassion and care for others, is snuffed out and the heart hardens like the wax of a cold candle. The deluge of abuse, abandoned wives and children, and the sorrow of divorce is the result of wickedness engulfing the world.

Today, sins of immorality run rampant, both secretly and openly. Abortions are not only increasing, but they are also being legalized, with no thought or natural parental feeling for the unborn. Pornography, sexual perversions, and abundant adulteries have led to broken hearts and homes. And often, through it all, the hearts of the wicked parties are cold and hardened to the sorrow they cause for those they should love. It is ironic that at a time when the peoples of the world should be turning their might to preparing for the coming of the Son of God to the earth to usher in peace and joy, many are racing toward hell and destruction. Again, is it any wonder that the Lord revealed that the last days are the days "of the end of the world, or the destruction of the wicked, which is the end of the world" (Joseph Smith—Matthew 1:4)? One is reminded of the awful situation of the Nephites. They reveled in iniquity until they became so hardened that the Spirit of the Lord ceased to strive with them and they ripened for destruction (see Mormon 3:12; 5:16).

Living in the Midst of Wickedness

As a young missionary, I noted with sadness the influence wickedness had on investigators accepting or rejecting the fulness of the gospel. On more than one occasion, we taught wonderful families who received our message, but when we would return to their homes, we'd learn that the fathers no longer wanted their family to listen to our message. In my naive youth, I could not understand why the father, who had earlier been so friendly with us and welcomed us into his home, would become so opposed to our teachings.

I recall one particular family we were teaching. We passed by the home during the week to continue contact while the father was on a business trip. The mother said she and her children had been reading the copy of the Book of Mormon we had left with them. I thought we had located a golden family, ready to become members of the Lord's Church. After the father returned home from his business trip, we again met with the family. His attitude had changed, and he openly declared that he did not believe in God or the Resurrection of Jesus Christ. I was shocked. When we visited with the family the next week, while the father was again on another business trip, the mother shared how she had hoped her husband would have felt the same way she did about our message. Finally, with tears in her eyes, she told us she knew her husband was an adulterer. She had hoped our message of faith and repentance would touch his heart and save their family.

In time, I have learned that when someone rejects the gospel, member or nonmember, it boils down to one question: which commandment is it that you do not want to keep? The Lord declared, "By this you may know they are under the bondage of sin, because they come not unto me. For whoso cometh not unto me is under the bondage of sin . . . And by this you may know the righteous from the wicked" (D&C 84:50–51, 53).

The Lord shared another reason for individuals rejecting the fulness of the gospel. "They turn their hearts from me," He explained, "because of the precepts of men" (D&C 45:29). The Book of Mormon prophet Nephi was blunt in elucidating the conditions of the last days. He expressed that "because of pride, and wickedness, and abominations, and whoredoms, they have all gone astray save it be a few, who are the humble followers of Christ; nevertheless, they are led, that in many instances they do err because they are taught by the precepts of men" (2 Nephi 28:14).

Elder Dallin H. Oaks described the state of affairs regarding the abounding iniquity in the last days. "Evil that used to be localized and covered like a boil is now legalized and paraded like a banner," he declared. "The most fundamental roots and bulwarks of civilization are questioned or attacked. Nations disavow their religious heritage.

Marriage and family responsibilities are discarded as impediments to personal indulgence. The movies and magazines and television that shape our attitudes are filled with stories or images that portray the children of God as predatory beasts or, at best, as trivial creations pursuing little more than personal pleasure. And too many of us accept this as entertainment."[35]

All peoples have the Light of Christ, which teaches them to know good from evil, invites them to do good, and persuades them to believe in Christ (see Moroni 7:16). Any individual who will not receive that light turns to darkness and the bondage of sin (see D&C 84:46–51). When an individual or group of people turn away from the Light of Christ and sear their conscience with wickedness, the Lord withdraws His Spirit and they lose the light they once had (see D&C 1:33).

The spiral down into darkness is like descending lower and lower into a pit, in which descent the individual or peoples become increasingly desperate and irrational. Historians recount the downfall of past societies because of their decline into wickedness. Written and unwritten biographies tell the story of individual destruction. This volume cannot duplicate the libraries of books telling the story of wickedness. However, a few select examples from the past that have been prophetically connected to the wickedness of the last days may be worthy of consideration.

Once again, let's take a few snapshots of specific time periods to illustrate the iniquity prophesied to precede the Savior's Second Coming: the days of Noah, the destruction of Jerusalem in AD 70, and the fall of the inhabitants of the Americas at the conclusion of each of the Book of Mormon societies—the Jaredites and the Nephites.

As It Was in the Days of Noah

In the Olivet Discourse, the Savior specifically cited the days of Noah: "But as it was in the days of Noah, so it shall be also at the coming of the Son of Man; for it shall be with them, as it was in the days which were before the flood; for until the day that Noah entered into the ark they were eating and drinking, marrying and giving in marriage; and they knew not until the flood came, and took them all away; so shall also the coming of the Son of Man be" (Joseph Smith—Matthew 1:41–43). Evidently, the wicked either simply reject or are oblivious to the prophecies and warnings of the last days.

In Noah's day, there were men who sought his life as he preached repentance (Moses 8:18). How extensive the devilish designs will become to take the lives of prophets in the last days is unknown. However, it is clear that at least two prophets will be killed because of the wickedness of those to whom they will preach (see Revelation 11:3–10). Further, our scant descriptions of the conditions in Noah's day paint a picture in which "every man was lifted in the imagination of the thoughts of his heart, being only evil continually" (Moses 8:22). They rejected the message of salvation through Jesus Christ and refused to hearken to Noah's message of faith, repentance, baptism, and the Holy Ghost (see Moses 8:24). Instead, they turned to filling the earth with violence and were ultimately destroyed by flood waters in their state of ripened iniquity (see Moses 8:28–30). As we shall see, violence and the disregard for human life has been and will be the end of a long but steep decline in society leading God to pour out His wrath to bring about society's destruction.

Abomination of Desolation: Iniquity of Meridian-Day Jerusalem and of the Last Days

The Savior also connected the wickedness at the time of His prophesied destruction of Jerusalem (the abomination of desolation) to the wickedness of the last days (see Joseph Smith—Matthew 1:10, 30). Although the conditions of latter-day wickedness should not come as news to anyone living in this time, a bit of reflection upon the Savior's direct correlation between the meridian day and the last days should illuminate the reality of our situation.

The grisly and gruesome details of abominations in Jerusalem prior to the city's destruction are beyond the scope of this work. The Roman/Jewish historian Josephus left a detailed account of that time. The Savior warned His disciples that any who saw the signs fulfilled concerning the destruction of Jerusalem were to flee Judea into the mountains. Even those on the housetops were to flee without entering their houses for their belongings or those in the fields to return for their clothes (Joseph Smith—Matthew 1:13–15). "For then, in those days," the Savior explained, "shall be great tribulation on the Jews, and upon the inhabitants of Jerusalem, such as was not before sent upon Israel, of God, since the beginning of their kingdom until this time" (Joseph Smith—Matthew 1:18). The destruction would be worse than that which befell

Jerusalem under the hands of the Babylonians six hundred years earlier. What iniquity could possibly merit such dire predictions? One might hope the Lord simply accentuated the warning with exaggeration, but unfortunately, such was not the case.

The choices that caused iniquity to abound and love to wax cold were not made in a single day but had been building for decades.[36] The religious leadership of the Jews had become corrupt to the point of crying out to Pilate, the Roman procurator, that the Son of God be crucified. The path that led to this depravity of soul included covetousness, in which chief priests, scribes, Sadducees, and Pharisees wallowed in lust and sought earthly acclaim and possessions above their care for God or man.

During His mortal ministry, the Savior called these religious leaders to repent of their hypocrisy. These wicked individuals hid behind a cloak of counterfeit righteousness, making conspicuous the outward signs of religious devotions among the Jews. In mocking gestures, they broadened their phylacteries, small boxes that contained passages from the Torah commanding Israel to "love the Lord thy God with all thine heart, and with all thy soul, and with all thy might" (Deuteronomy 6:5, 8). These sacred objects were placed over the forehead and left upper arm, near the heart. In addition, the Savior noted that they enlarged the borders of their garments, referring to the tassels of their tallith (Matthew 23:5), a type of shawl with fringes, that were to help them "remember all the commandments of the Lord, and do them" (Numbers 15:39). Yet, these religious leaders of the apostate Jewish nation were full of greed and self-indulgence (Matthew 23:25).

Consider the few insights into their hearts from the records of the New Testament. The Savoir described the scribes on the one hand as having a "desire to walk in long robes, [who] love greetings in the markets, and the highest seats in the synagogues, and the chief rooms as feasts . . . and for a shew make long prayers," while on the other hand, they "devour widows' houses" (Luke 20:46–47). In particular, they discarded the sacred covenant of marriage and turned it into a means of hiding their lustful adulteries. Marriage, divorce, and remarriage became a means of moving from wife to wife as they indulged their lust, free of cultural disapproval. The Savior's words to the Pharisees reveal the irony of them being religious leaders: "O fools! For you have said in your hearts, There is no God. And you pervert the right way; and the kingdom of heaven suffereth violence of you; and you persecute the meek; and in your violence you seek to destroy the kingdom; and ye take the children of the kingdom by force. Woe unto you, ye adulterers" (JST, Luke 16:21). Christ's greatest condemnation was for the sin of hypocrisy (see Matthew 23). He repetitively emphasized that His denunciation of the scribes and Pharisees centered on their hypocritical insincerity, which President J. Reuben Clark Jr. described as "the living of the double life, the life we let our friends and sometimes our wives believe, and the life we actually live."[37]

We live without knowing how far down the road current societal conditions will lead before the wicked are destroyed. In the case of meridian-day iniquity, the disregard for widows and marriage covenants, hypocrisy of clergy covering their immoralities, and atheistic philosophies that justified wickedness were only a few steps toward filling society's cup with sin and vice. As aforementioned, the conditions of wickedness spiraled further downward until "because of their iniquities, and the hardness of their hearts, and the stiffness of their necks" (2 Nephi 25:12), they were willing to crucify the Son of God.

It seems to be appropriate to note that today the vile comments concerning Christ and religion on the Internet in general and mainstream news outlets approach the hatred of the meridian-day Jewish leaders for Christ and His teachings. The attacks on God, Christ, and religion have become common and increasingly more vile. Religious leaders in the news have not necessarily helped the cause of faith. They have gone so far as to denounce others' religions, support and participate in immoral acts, and lead people away from the simplest, purest doctrines of Christ.

Again, the same things happening today happened in Christ's day. And if those acts had been the end of the story of depravity for the meridian-day Jews, we might conclude that we in the last days have reached the bottom of the pit of decadence and are equal to them. Unfortunately, their story continues and gives us further cause for reflection and warning.

In the decades that followed the Son of God's crucifixion, the need to revive obedience to God's laws became evident; however, that need was taken to the other extreme of wickedness—oppressing any who did not live according to the required religious zeal. Those who called themselves Zealots sought to defend the laws of God and oppose the oppressive rule of the Romans. In place of the Roman rule, they imposed their brand of religion upon the people by overthrowing the incompetent leaders appointed by the Romans and taking charge of the government.

As the Savior prophesied, there arose many false prophets and false Messiahs willing to lead the Jews (Joseph Smith—Matthew 1:9, 22). The Romans' fierce attempts to quell multiple insurrections gave rise to bitter extremist political resistance. The major opposition came from a group of terrorists who called themselves the *Sicarii*. Like a modern drug cartel or gang, the *Sicarii* specialized in secretive killings to further their interests. They derived their name from the dagger or blade of an assassin, the *sicai*.[38] Richard Draper has written regarding the growing influence of the *Sicarii*: "Throughout Judea, Galilee and its northeastern neighbor, Gaulanitis, the *Sicarii* made a large number of recruits. . . . Fearlessly, they burned and plundered at will, claiming that all who did not assist them were sympathizers of Rome."[39] The Jewish historian, Josephus, reported that the influence of the *Sicarii* spread to Jerusalem and inflicted "worse atrocities"on the Jews than did the Romans.[40] Local government leaders joined hands with the *Sicarii* and accepted their plunder in return for protection. Jealousy and fighting between various groups of Zealots, legitimately appointed government leaders, Jewish religious leaders, including the high priest and his family, and the powerful *Sicarii* left Jerusalem in the hands of robbers and murderers. The *Sicarii* delighted in plunder and bloodshed to sustain their wickedness and lust for power. Even these fought among themselves and sought to demonstrate how fierce they could be by inflicting greater and greater atrocities. Josephus recorded that one band from Galilee, led by John of Gishala, turned the city of Jerusalem into a mocking butcher's shop. "Their passion for looting was insatiable," Josephus recounted. "They ransacked rich men's houses, murdered men and violated women for sport."[41]

A similar description of latter-day outrages has thus far been restricted to what might be considered third-world countries and those ravaged by drug cartels. Their tales are so shocking that they leave listeners incredulous and unable to fully comprehend the realities of the iniquity that abounds when love waxes cold.

Nevertheless, this is not the end of the tale. Josephus continues his narrative and relates that these bands of robbers "shamelessly gave themselves up to effeminate practices, adorning their hair and putting on women's clothes, steeping themselves in scent [perfumes] and painting under their eyes to make themselves attractive. They copied not merely the dress but also the passions of women, and in their utter filthiness invented unlawful pleasures; they wallowed in slime, turning the whole city into a brothel and polluting it with the foulest practices. Yet though they had the faces of women, they had the hands of murderers; they approached with mincing steps, then in a flash became fighting-men, and drawing their swords from under their dyed cloaks ran every passer-by through."42

Is it any wonder that the Lord stood back as the Roman armies under Titus cleansed Jerusalem and the temple of such wickedness? It was like the great flood, removing the wicked from this one corrupt place; however, this time, the Roman sword came as the deluge upon the wicked. Again, is it any wonder that in the last days, when similar iniquity occurs, the very angels of heaven "are crying unto the Lord day and night, who are ready and waiting to be sent forth to reap down the fields" (D&C 86:5)? It seems proper to recall that in the Savior's discourse on the Mount of Olives He emphasized that in the last days, "*again,* because iniquity shall abound; the love of men shall wax cold; but he that shall not be overcome, the same shall be saved" (Joseph Smith—Matthew 1:30; emphasis added). The Savior's words first were restricted to the wickedness of those in Jerusalem; the reiteration of these same conditions of wickedness as signs of His coming may apply to a broader geography. Therefore, we must not be surprised to hear of similar atrocities in our lifetime. On the other hand, it is also necessary that we not only refrain from wickedness but also reach out to the victims of wickedness and, if possible, prevent such evil from finding more victims.

Book of Mormon Warning: Secret Combinations of Wickedness

An additional witness of the iniquity that exists in the last days is found in the prophetic warnings and historical accounts of the wicked Jaredite and Nephite societies in the Book of Mormon. The prophet Mormon testified that the Lord commanded him to write to the Gentiles of the last days, "Repent of your evil doings, of your lyings and deceivings, and your whoredoms, and of your secret abominations, and your idolatries, and of your murders, and your priestcrafts, and your envyings, and your strifes, and from all your wickedness and abominations" (3 Nephi 30:2). The strongest forewarnings in the Book of Mormon describe the downfall of entire societies because of secret combinations established among the people.

The name *Gadianton* brings to mind one "who was exceedingly expert in many words, and also in his craft, to carry on the secret work of murder and of robbery" (Helaman 2:4). His teachings are attributed to proving "the overthrow, yea, almost the entire destruction of the people of Nephi" (Helaman 2:13). Similar to the *Sicarii* of ancient Jerusalem, Gadianton organized bands of robbers and murderers who united to carry out their wicked designs. Further, they infiltrated the government "and did enter into their covenants and their oaths, that they would protect and preserve one another in whatsoever difficult circumstances they should be placed, that they should not suffer for their murders, and their plunderings, and their stealings" (Helaman 6:21). Eventually, "they did obtain the sole management of the government . . . that they might get gain and glory of the world, and, moreover, that they might the more easily commit adultery, and steal, and kill, and do according to their own wills" (Helaman 6:39; 7:5).

Nephi warned that there would be secret combinations like those that destroyed the Jaredite and the Nephite societies among the Gentiles in the last days (2 Nephi 26:14, 22). In the latter part of the twentieth century, both Presidents Ezra Taft Benson and Gordon B. Hinckley warned of the secret combinations that existed in the world during the time of their ministry. "I testify that wickedness is rapidly expanding in every segment of our society," President Benson declared. "It is more highly organized, more cleverly disguised, and more powerfully promoted than ever before. Secret combinations lusting for power, gain, and glory are flourishing. A secret combination that seeks to overthrow the freedom of all lands, nations, and countries is increasing its evil influence and control over America and the entire world (see Ether 8:18–25)."[43] Apparently in prophetic wisdom, President Benson did not identify any specific entity as the secret combination to which he referred. I recall my questions at the time President Benson spoke; was this communism, socialism, drug cartels, or some other powerful movement?

Today, I only have more questions. Has the evil that President Benson referred to been stopped? Is the secret combination of wickedness an extreme Muslim terrorist organization, bankers and Wall Street machinations that seek to gain wealth, increasingly powerful drug and human trafficking cartels, mafia, pornography brokers, the incessant drum beating out the message of same gender, bisexual, transgender proponents in the courts and political arenas, socialism, some political agenda—or all of these? It may not be known until the day that "their iniquities shall be spoken upon the housetops, and their secret acts shall be revealed" (D&C 1:3) that we will know with surety and entirety the wickedness hidden in secret combinations to which President Benson referred.

In like manner, less than a month after the events of September 11, 2001, President Hinckley addressed the Church regarding the identification of Al Qaeda and its protectorate in Afghanistan, the Taliban. "We of this Church know something of such groups," President Hinckley remarked. "The Book of Mormon speaks of the Gadianton robbers, a vicious, oath-bound, and secret organization bent on evil and destruction. In their day they did all in their power, by whatever means available, to bring down the Church, to woo the people with sophistry, and to take control of the society. We see the same thing in the present situation."[44]

On a similar warning note, Elder M. Russell Ballard taught:

> The Book of Mormon teaches that secret combinations engaged in crime present a serious challenge, not just to individuals and families but to entire civilizations. Among today's secret combinations are gangs, drug cartels, and organized crime families. The secret combinations of our day function much like the Gadianton robbers of the Book of Mormon times. They have secret signs and code words. They participate in secret rites and initiation ceremonies. Among their purposes are to "murder, and plunder, and steal, and commit whoredoms and all manner of wickedness, contrary to the laws of their country and also the laws of their God" (Helaman 6:23).
>
> If we are not careful, today's secret combinations can obtain power and influence just as quickly and just as completely as they did in Book of Mormon times. Do you remember the pattern? The secret combinations began among the "more wicked part" of society, but eventually "seduced the more part of the righteous" until the whole society was polluted [Helaman 6:38].[45]

Opposition to the Restoration of the Gospel

A portion of the wickedness of the last days is specifically aimed at the Restoration of the gospel and The Church of Jesus Christ of Latter-day Saints. This last dispensation is the final bastion to threaten Lucifer, his followers, and their kingdom of wickedness. In the beginning of the

Restoration, it became evident that Satan was aware of God's work being planted on the earth. As a type of forewarning concerning the opposition that would be raised against the Lord's people, Satan sought to overcome the young Joseph Smith with darkness when he first prayed in the grove of trees near his home. Three years later, Moroni informed Joseph that his "name should be had for good and evil among all nations, kindreds, and tongues, or that it should be both good and evil spoken of among all people" (Joseph Smith—History 1:33). When the Prophet received instruction following his disobedience in allowing Martin Harris to take one hundred and sixteen manuscript pages of translation, which were lost, the Lord warned that Satan would attempt to keep men from having light pierce the darkness of the Apostasy. "Satan will harden the hearts of the people to stir them up to anger against you," Christ revealed, "that they will not believe my words. Thus Satan thinketh to overpower your testimony in this generation, that the work may not come forth in this generation" (D&C 10:32–33).

Not only was the Prophet Joseph forewarned as he worked to unfold the kingdom of God on earth, but the prophets of old were forewarned that this latter-day work would meet opposition. An angel showed Nephi that the Saints of the last days would be persecuted by the great and abominable church, which would have dominion over all the earth. Nephi "beheld the church of the Lamb of God, and its numbers were few, because of the wickedness and abominations of the whore that sat upon many waters; nevertheless," Nephi further recorded, "I beheld that the church of the Lamb, who were the saints of God, were also upon all the face of the earth; and their dominions upon the face of the earth were small, because of the wickedness of the great whore whom I saw. And it came to pass that I beheld that the great mother of abominations did gather together multitudes upon the face of the earth, among all the nations of the Gentiles, to fight against the Lamb of God" (1 Nephi 14:12–13).

We have not yet taken the message of the Restoration to all nations. But what the future will hold with regard to the opposition the Saints will experience when that day comes will most likely be equal to the faith of those who will accept the glad tidings of the Restoration of the gospel. We have some insight from past and current opposition marshaled to prevent the building of each temple in this last dispensation. When encouraging the Saints to build the Salt Lake Temple, President Brigham Young referred to the always present opposition to temples: "Some say, 'I do not like to do it, for we never began to build a Temple without the bells of hell beginning to ring.'" President Young continued, "I want to hear them ring again."

Following that bold declaration, he recounted the mobbing and persecutions that had been heaped upon the Saints in the past, and then he asked, "What did they accomplish? They magnified the work of the Lord in the eyes of the nations. . . . Some of the brethren are all the time foreseeing evil that the Saints are going to suffer, and saying that we are going to see harder times than ever before, and that the armies . . . of the nations will yet gather against us. Let them gather: the Lord will perform his work."[46]

Nephi also bore testimony that all the efforts of the wicked will not stop the work of God within or without The Church of Jesus Christ of Latter-day Saints. He testified that he "beheld the power of the Lamb of God, that it descended upon the saints of the church of the Lamb, and upon the covenant people of the Lord, who were scattered upon the face of all the earth; and they were armed with righteousness and with the power of God in great glory" (1 Nephi 14:14). The consequences of the wickedness among the nations will be that they war among themselves and "the wrath of God [will be] poured out upon the mother of harlots, which is the great and abominable church of all the earth, whose founder is the devil" (1 Nephi 14:17).

Is the World Wicked Enough Yet?

On occasion, I have heard individuals ask in despair, "How much more wicked must the world become before the Lord will return?" The inference is that the Savior cannot return until wickedness increases beyond that which is currently on the earth. It is almost as if one is putting words into the Lord's mouth, such as, "If only the people would become more wicked, I could return. I wonder how much longer until they will really be wicked." In one of the earliest revelations following the organization of the Church, the Lord made a very relevant declaration. As you read His statement, see if you can fill in the missing word: "The field . . . is white already to be . . . ?" Did you suggest that the missing word should be *harvested*? On most occasions in the Doctrine and Covenants, that would be correct. However, while addressing Thomas B. Marsh, the Savior declared that "the field is . . . white ready . . . to be *burned*" (D&C 31:4; emphasis added)!

I understand this to mean that in 1830 the earth was already ripened and sufficiently wicked to be burned. In other words, the Lord has not been nor is He waiting for wickedness to worsen before He returns. The lack of greater wickedness is not preventing the Lord from returning in glory. The wickedness is in place. Rather, it appears that the timing of the Second Coming is more closely correlated with work that the righteous need to fulfill, a topic we will discuss in a later chapter when we touch on that theme.

4
TRIBULATIONS OF THE LAST DAYS

As aforementioned, one of the three main themes in Enoch's revelations concerning the last days is that of tribulations. There is a correlation between the wickedness of the earth in general and the conditions of the last days. John the Revelator saw the symbolic pouring out of the wrath of God upon the wicked as liquid being poured out upon the earth.

The Lord identified tribulations, such as tempests, earthquakes, hailstorms, famines, and pestilences, as voices by which He calls upon the inhabitants of the earth to repent of their wickedness (see D&C 43:25). Further, the Lord declared, "I have sworn in my wrath, and decreed wars upon the face of the earth" (D&C 63:33). President Joseph F. Smith explained,

> We believe that his judgments are poured out to bring mankind to a sense of his power and his purposes, that they may repent of their sins and prepare themselves for the second coming of Christ to reign in righteousness on the earth. . . . We believe that these severe, natural calamities are visited upon men by the Lord for the good of his children, to quicken their devotion to others, and to bring out their better natures, that they may love and serve him. We believe, further, that they are the heralds and tokens of his final judgment, and the schoolmasters to teach the people to prepare themselves by righteous living for the coming of the Savior to reign upon the earth, when every knee shall bow and every tongue confess that Jesus is the Christ.[47]

Much of the purpose of tribulations in the last days is connected to people's cold, hardened hearts. While many individuals respond to the Spirit that guides them to walk in paths of righteousness, others become deaf to the promptings of the Spirit. Similar to Laman and Lemuel in the Book of Mormon, we might say of the wicked that God has spoken and will speak to them "in a still small voice" but that they are "past feeling. . . . Wherefore, he has spoken unto [them] like unto the voice of thunder" (1 Nephi 17:45). The tribulations of the last days are like the words of Lehi to his wayward sons when he feared they would be cast off from the presence of the Lord. "He did exhort them then with all the feeling of a tender parent, that they would hearken to his words, that perhaps the Lord would be merciful to them, and not cast them off" (1 Nephi 8:37). Through tribulations, Heavenly Father is calling us back to Him with all the feeling of a tender parent so we will not be cast off from Him in the end.

Many of the tribulations of the last days have been revealed in symbolic terms. The Apostle John saw and heard seven angels sound trumps announcing conditions of the last days (Revelation 8–11). Subsequently, the Lord referred to further tribulations as "the day when the wrath of God shall be poured out upon the wicked without measure" (D&C 1:9). The Lord likened His wrath unto a liquid in a vessel that is poured out upon the earth as plagues, pestilences, earthquakes, etc. (see Revelation 16). However, the tribulations are not to be seen simply as punishments poured out upon the wicked. Rather, tribulations start as trumpeting voices of warning that are only later repeated and magnified as they are poured out as destructive punishments on the wicked. Ultimately, they are signs that mortal probation upon the earth is about to come to an end.

This stage of the plan of salvation will be fulfilled, and the time of mortal probation will be completed. Those who do not repent will lament. "The harvest is past, the summer is ended, and my soul is not saved" (D&C 56:16). When they die, the wicked receive an incredible wake-up call for eternity. The end of their mortal probation and subsequent judgment to remain in spirit prison will surely give them cause to reconsider the course they were pursuing.

The tribulations may be viewed as a precursor to the great, last day when the earth will be cleansed of all wickedness. "For the day soon cometh that all the proud and they who do wickedly shall be as stubble; and the day cometh that they must be burned" (1 Nephi 22:15). Tribulations do not bring the end of the world but, instead, warn that the end is near.

Storms and Tempests of the Last Days

The Lord clearly forewarned that those living in the last days will live in a time of many tribulations. These tribulations have been, are, and will be real. They make up the fabric of life on earth in the last days. There is no need to dwell on each challenge individually, but a review of the Lord's words may be helpful. In proper context, the tribulations of the last days are but part of the larger scheme of the Lord's plan. He declared that He has called upon His children "by the mouth of my servants, and by the ministering of angels, and by mine own voice" (D&C 43:25). In addition, the Lord revealed that He calls upon the earth's inhabitants by the voice of thunderings, lightnings, tempests, earthquakes, great hailstorms, famines, and pestilences of every kind (see D&C 43:25). To this list, the Lord added, "The voice of the waves of the sea [heave] themselves beyond their bounds" (D&C 88:90).

We have some idea about what the realizations of these warnings will mean to those who experience them. Elder Quentin L. Cook related his own and others' thoughts and experiences following numerous fulfillments of these prophesied tribulations:

> We are preparing for the Second Coming of the Savior. The scriptures are clear that no one knows when this will occur. The scriptures do tell us that in the last days, among the bitter cups we will face, there will be "earthquakes, in divers places" and the "waves of the sea heaving themselves beyond their bounds" [Matthew 24:7; D&C 88:90; Joseph Smith—Matthew 1:29].
>
> Devastating earthquakes and tsunamis have recently occurred in diverse places, including Chile, Haiti, and the islands of the Pacific. A few weeks ago Presiding Bishop H. David Burton, Elder Tad R. Callister, and I were able to meet with the Saints who had lost family members as a result of the tsunami that hit the eastern side of Samoa last September. The chapel was full, and it was an emotional meeting. We were able to assure these choice members that because of the Atonement of Jesus Christ, they can be reunited with the loved ones they have lost.

The stake president, Sonny Purcell, was driving his car when he saw the enormous wave coming far out at sea. He honked his horn and stopped children on the road walking to school and warned them to run for higher ground and safety as fast as they could. The children followed his instruction. He frantically drove, reached his four-year-old daughter, put her in the car, and then tried to get to his mother. Before he could reach his mother, the wall of water picked up his car and swept it over 100 yards (91 m), where it lodged in a tree. He scrambled to secure his daughter on top of the car and then swam to rescue his mother, who was clinging to a branch of another tree near their house. With great effort he swam with her to the car and safety. Many were not as fortunate. They did not have time to get to higher ground and safety. Many lost their lives, particularly the young and the elderly.

We told the Samoan families that members all over the world expressed love and concern and had prayed for them and contributed fast offerings and humanitarian aid for both the members and their neighbors. The same is true for the members and their neighbors in Chile and Haiti. We do this because we follow Jesus Christ.[48]

As one reads or listens to such accounts, what earlier might have been a wild imagination of the last days begins to come to life and become reality. These events no longer remain in the sphere of fireside topics or classes with sensational discussions. The prophesied tribulations of the last days are happening in our day. They are not something to be feared, but they are conditions in which we can comfort and strengthen one another with preparatory prevention, humanitarian aid, and testimony.

An Overflowing Scourge and Desolating Sickness

The Lord specifically mentioned that those living in the last days will "see an overflowing scourge; for a desolating sickness shall cover the land" (D&C 45:31). Naturally, each time a potential epidemic rears its head, we ask ourselves if this could be the fulfillment of the Lord's words. The influenza epidemic at the turn of the twentieth century surely fits the description given by the Lord; so do the smallpox and AIDS epidemics. But rather than look for one specific disease to fulfill the prophecy, it appears that the intent of the Savior's words was to point to epidemic sickness that would afflict the world's inhabitants at various times. The ongoing scourge also serves as a voice to call people to repentance. "For a desolating scourge shall go forth among the inhabitants of the earth," the Savior warned, "and shall continue to be poured out from time to time, if they repent not, until the earth is empty, and the inhabitants thereof are consumed away and utterly destroyed by the brightness of my coming" (D&C 5:19). The clarification that this prophesied scourge will continue to come upon the earth informs us that it may be a wiser course to note many fulfillments of this condition of the last days rather than look for one grand fulfillment.

Years ago, when the scourge of AIDS first spread upon the earth, the First Presidency issued a statement for the membership of the Church. Its message is particularly pertinent, as it provides prophetic guidance and counsel for the last days concerning a desolating scourge of our times.

> We call your attention to President Gordon B. Hinckley's remarks . . . given in the April 1987 General Priesthood Meeting: . . .
>
> "Each of us has a choice between right and wrong. But with that choice there inevitably will follow consequences. Those who choose to violate the commandments of God put themselves at great spiritual and physical jeopardy. . . .
>
> "We plead with people everywhere to live in accordance with the teachings of our Creator and rise above carnal attractions that often result in the tragedies that follow moral transgression. . . .
>
> "Having said this, I desire now to say with emphasis that our concern for the bitter fruit of sin is coupled with Christlike sympathy for its victims, innocent or culpable. We advocate the example of the Lord, who condemned the sin, yet loved the sinner. We should reach out with kindness and comfort to the afflicted, ministering to their needs and assisting them with their problems. We repeat, however, that the way of safety and the road to happiness lie in abstinence before marriage and fidelity following marriage." (*Ensign*, May 1987, 46–47)
>
> Members of the Church should extend compassion to those who are ill. . . . We express great love and sympathy

for all victims but particularly those who [have innocently contracted a disease]. In the Lord's eternal plan, those who endure such suffering, pain, and injustice, not of their own doing, will receive compensatory blessings through the Lord's infinite mercy. . . .

The Lord has not left mankind without clear guidance on matters that affect our happiness. That guidance is chastity before marriage, total fidelity in marriage, abstinence from all homosexual relations, avoidance of illegal drugs, and reverence and care for the body, which is the "temple of God." (1 Cor. 3:16)[49]

Among the many insights we might gain from a review of that timely counsel, two that stand out are that throughout the time of scourges and desolating sicknesses, there is a need to reach out to their victims and find means to eradicate the offending diseases, and that living the gospel is the best course to follow.

Joseph Smith clarified that the Saints will also succumb to the diseases and sicknesses because of the weakness of the flesh. He wrote that he

explained concerning the coming of the Son of Man; also that it is a false idea that the Saints will escape all the judgments, whilst the wicked suffer; for all flesh is subject to suffer, and "the righteous shall hardly escape"; still many of the Saints will escape, for the just shall live by faith; yet many of the righteous shall fall a prey to disease, to pestilence, etc., by reason of the weakness of the flesh, and yet be saved in the Kingdom of God. So that it is an unhallowed principle to say that such and such have transgressed because they have been preyed upon by disease or death, for all flesh is subject to death; and the Savior has said, "Judge not, lest ye be judged."[50]

Significantly, the desolations of the last days are not free to run rampant without any divine restraint or control. Neither are their purposes to destroy the earth and its people. One item often passed over is the use of the term "a third part" that is associated with the desolations enumerated in the revelation of John the Apostle. When the seven angels are each handed a trump to announce the tribulations of the last days, five of them declare destruction of a third part of trees, grass, the sea, rivers, the sun, moon, stars, and men. The term "a third part is a rabbinism expressing a considerable number."[51] Nevertheless, the term also indicates that it is a plague with bounds God has set; all of the earth is not destroyed, but a specified remnant of the earth is affected—a third part. "So," Richard Draper explained, "the fraction John gives suggests that the purpose of the destruction in Revelation 8 is not so much retribution as a last attempt to turn man to God."[52]

Wars Prophesied to Precede the Second Coming

The concept of war did not begin with events in the last days. Not only have nations warred against one another since the creation of nations, but empires have also risen and fallen. The latter-day interest in wars is that the Savior indicated wars would continue to exist and even spread to include all of the nations of the earth. Note the Savior's very simple wording in describing the last days as a time when the elect, specifically those who gather to the restoration of His church and gospel, "shall hear of wars, and rumors of wars. Behold I speak for mine elect's sake; for nation shall rise against nation, and kingdom against kingdom" (Joseph Smith—Matthew 1:28–29).

For those living during the beginning of the Restoration, it must have come as a shock to learn that even the United States would divide in war, with states aligning themselves against one another. The first divine indication of this came in March 1831. "Ye hear of wars in foreign lands," the Savior began, "but, behold, I say unto you, they are nigh, even at your doors, and not many years hence ye shall hear of wars in your own lands" (D&C 45:63). The Lord instructed the Saints to gather in the western countries and establish "a city of refuge, a place of safety for the Saints of the Most High God" (D&C 45:66). Later events unfolded to manifest that ideally the aforementioned city would be the New Jerusalem, with its center emanating from Independence, Jackson County, Missouri. However, the Saints lacked the unity and faithful obedience necessary to create a Zion society (see D&C 101:1–8; 105:1–5), and consequently, they were driven from Jackson County and, eventually, from Missouri and then Illinois, until they settled in the Rocky Mountains. Thus, when the prophesied wars began "at the rebellion of South Carolina" and spread to a time when "the Southern States [were] divided against the Northern States" (D&C 87:1, 3), most of the Saints had gathered far away from the devastation of that conflict.

The Saints of the nineteenth century knew that following the Civil War in the United States the time would soon come when war would be poured out upon all nations. The twentieth century was home to two world wars, and war continues to spread from nation to nation and kingdom to kingdom as the decades pass without hope for true peace. That in itself is an important message in the Savior's Olivet Discourse—that is, the promised millennial era of peace will not be ushered in because individuals in nations and cultures will learn to live in harmony but because the wicked of the world will be destroyed to assure that war will cease.

War is the result of wickedness. Desire to possess property and the spirit of covetousness have powerful influence on the hearts of men. When the Lord commanded and instructed the Saints to establish Zion, He revealed that they were to purchase the lands of their inheritance and explained, "That you may have advantage of the world, that you may have claim on the world, that they may not be stirred up unto anger. For Satan putteth it into their hearts to anger against you, and to the shedding of blood" (D&C 63:27–28). Of the many lessons we might learn studying the Book of Mormon war chapters, one is that wicked individuals move societies to clash in war. For example, Mormon recorded that after the dissenting Nephites (known as Amalekites and Zoramites) united themselves with the Lamanites, Zerahemnah appointed them as his chief captains over the Lamanite armies because they "were of a more wicked and murderous disposition than the Lamanites were" (Alma 43:6). Later, Mormon identified the wicked Nephite dissenter Amalickiah as the cause of destruction and war among the Nephites and Lamanites, emphasizing "the great wickedness one very wicked man can cause to take place among the children of men" (Alma 46:9). In assessing the cause of wars, Mormon summarized, "For it has been their quarrelings and their contentions, yea, their murderings, and their plunderings, their idolatry, their whoredoms, and their abominations, which were among themselves, which brought upon them their wars and their destructions" (Alma 50:21).

One war-associated word captures the end of the era of the last days and the destruction of millions on the earth—*Armageddon!* John the Revelator saw that "the spirits of devils, working miracles, which go forth unto the kings of the earth and of the whole world, to gather them to the battle of that great day of God Almighty. . . . And he gathered them together into a place called in the Hebrew tongue Armageddon" (Revelation 16:14, 16). From that one revelatory passage at the end of the New Testament, we anticipate that all wars will culminate in the Jezreel Valley in the Lower Galilee region of Palestine. The events of war surrounding Armageddon will be discussed further in the chapter on signs of the last hours. It seems altogether fitting that an ultimate war, which began when Lucifer and his hosts rebelled in heaven, would find its way into the last days as a final manifestation of wickedness.

5

EARTHQUAKES, WARS, FAMINES, AND DISEASE: WHY ARE THE RIGHTEOUS NOT SPARED?

INDIVIDUALS LIVING IN THE LAST days are faced with penetrating and oftentimes disturbing issues of evil and suffering. And it's easy to question, why does God not intervene to save those who suffer what seem to be premature or agonizing deaths due to war, earthquakes, fires, hurricanes, tsunamis, and disease? Since God foreknows and has foretold the tribulations of the last days, why does He not cut the time shorter to prevent horrific wars and natural disasters or eradicate poverty and disease?

These questions come into greater focus when one considers that the Lord declared that in the midst of the tribulations of the last days, "men's hearts shall fail them, and they shall say that Christ delayeth his coming until the end of the earth" (D&C 45:26). In despair, "among the wicked, men shall lift up their voices and curse God and die" (D&C 45:32).

Elder M. Russell Ballard stated, "One cannot look at suffering, regardless of its causes or origins, without feeling pain and compassion. I can understand why someone who lacks an eternal perspective might see the horrifying news footage of starving children and man's inhumanity to man and shake a fist at the heavens and cry, 'If there is a God, how could he allow such things to happen?'"[53] When he was a member of the Quorum of the Twelve Apostles, Spencer W. Kimball addressed the Church regarding the Lord's involvement in causing or preventing death and suffering. Concerning these issues, he readily acknowledged, "Answer, if you can. I cannot, for though I know God has a major role in our lives, I do not know how much he causes to happen and how much he merely permits. Whatever the answer to this question, there is another I feel sure about. Could the Lord have prevented these tragedies? The answer is, Yes. The Lord is omnipotent, with all power to control our lives, save us pain, prevent all accidents, drive all planes and cars, feed us, protect us, save us from labor, effort, sickness, even from death, if he will. But he will not."[54]

To put it briefly, the answer to the stated concerns is that God does not intervene because in His divine wisdom, He knows that such intervention would not be in our best eternal interests and also because if we turn to Him, He can and will enable us to overcome all of the negative effects caused by such sufferings. Regarding the miseries and travails of the Saints as they were driven from the state of Missouri and the Prophet Joseph Smith's illegal imprisonment in Liberty Jail, the Lord assured, "Know thou, my son, that all these things shall give thee experience, and shall be for thy good" (D&C 122:7). At an earlier time, the Lord reassured, "Let your hearts be comforted; for all things will work together for good to them that walk uprightly" (D&C 100:15; see also D&C 90:24; 105:40).

One of my daughters frequently expresses her wish that the Second Coming already be here so she can live in a millennial state of peace without earthly cares. She longs to be in the presence of God. I have lovingly reminded her that, along with Adam and Eve, we chose the plan by which we would not come to earth to spend our lives in the Garden of Eden. True, living in the last days of mortality has its challenges, but there is reason in its design.

The Divine Paradigm

Although we are not able to fully comprehend God and all His ways, He has revealed enough of His purposes to give answers and insights to our most penetrating questions regarding the tribulations of the last days. He does not view mortality in the same manner many of us do. It might be said that, in comparison with the various theories of man, the Lord's perspective is the *divine paradigm*. The Lord sees the challenges of mortality and living in the last days through the lense of eternal purpose. Our understanding of the Lord's perspective is couched in the plan of salvation. This plan reveals that there is godly design in mortality, even with its attendant evils and suffering.

We were begotten as spirit children of Heavenly Parents and lived with them before we came to earth. Mortality is but a fraction of our existence as we become more like our Heavenly Parents. The time most mortals spend on this earth is brief, at best, in relation to the eons of time we spent learning and becoming as premortal spirit beings. Likewise, an eternity of future existence stretches out before us.

Next, the key to understanding God's intervention (or seeming lack thereof) and the purposes of mortality lies in our understanding of how the Atonement of Jesus Christ is woven into our existence. Heavenly Father used divine design to plan mortality, including salvation from the ills and wickedness of this present existence through the atoning sacrifice of the Only Begotten Son of God. That is, mortality, with its attendant wickedness, tribulations, wars, suffering, and death, was never intended to stand alone without means of deliverance from its inevitable death, suffering, and evil. Through the Atonement, mortality becomes not just a moment in time but an actual connecting piece of eternity. Thus, "if we looked at mortality as the whole of existence, then pain, sorrow, failure, and short life would be calamity," President Spencer W. Kimball explained. "But if we look upon life as an eternal thing stretching far into the premortal past and on into the eternal post-death future, then all happenings may be put in proper perspective."[55]

God the Father provided and explained to us mortality's purposes and attendant bounds and guidelines before we were born on earth, and we sanctioned them.[56] One of the purposes of our mortal existence is that we are here as part of an ongoing process of perfection, in which we are tested, tried, and refined (see Abraham 3:25; Job 23:10; Isaiah 48:10; D&C 136:31).

The Refiner's Fire

"But who may abide the day of his coming?" the prophet Malachi asked. "And who shall stand when he appeareth? for he is like a refiner's fire . . . and he shall sit as a refiner and purifier of silver . . . and purge them as gold and silver" (Malachi 3:2–3). The Lord seeks to further purify and purge His children of their sins and weaknesses, like a refiner's fire purges gold and silver of their impurities, and He does it so these experiences will serve for their education in the eternities.[57] The refining process for ore includes pressure, heat, and time. Mortality's refining process purposefully includes tribulations, diseases, wars, earthquakes, persecutions, disappointments, enduring, and more, for these are the means, as deemed by God, to best purify His children. The Apostle Peter admonished the Saints of his day, "Beloved, think it not strange concerning the fiery trial which is to try you, as though some strange thing happened unto you" (1 Peter 4:12). A Chinese proverb states that true gold does not fear the refiner's fire. There is an important lesson in the fact that although the Lord could deliver us from the tribulations and challenges of the last days, He does not.

The Tribulations of the Last Days Test and Increase Faith

The events of the last days were designed to test and help increase faith. If God intervened to rescue the innocent from suffering, they would not develop the faith they would need in the eternities. Elder Robert D. Hales taught:

> We realize that the purpose of our life on earth is to grow, develop, and be strengthened through our own experiences. How do we do this? The scriptures give us an answer in one simple phrase: we "wait upon the Lord" (Psalm 37:9; 123:2; Isaiah 8:17; 40:31; 2 Nephi 18:17). Tests and trials are given to all of us. These mortal challenges allow us and our Heavenly Father to see whether we will exercise our agency to follow His Son. He already knows, and we have the opportunity to learn, that no matter how difficult our circumstances, "all these things shall [be for our] experience, and . . . [our] good" (D&C 122:7).
>
> Does this mean we will always understand our challenges? Won't all of us, sometime, have reason to ask, "O God, where art thou" (D&C 121:1)? Yes! When a spouse dies, a companion will wonder. When financial hardship befalls a family, a father or mother will ask. When children wander from the path, a mother and father will cry out in sorrow. Yes, "weeping may endure for a night, but joy cometh in the morning" (Psalm 30:5). Then, in the dawn of our increased faith and understanding, we arise and choose to wait upon the Lord, saying, "Thy will be done" (Matthew 6:10; 3 Nephi 13:10; see also Matthew 26:39).[58]

Perhaps more important than the test we face of retaining our faith that God exists are the circumstances that test and strengthen our faith that He is interested in our eternal happiness and that we can truly trust Him even when faced with uncertainties and paradoxes that seem to defy our understanding of God's purposes.

One occasion that provides insight into the Lord's hand being in the seemingly paradoxical tests and tribulations of life is the episode in Church history known as Zion's Camp. In February 1834, the Lord called for the Saints to raise an army to act under the direction of the Prophet Joseph Smith. The immediate goal appeared to be that of redeeming the Saints' land in Jackson County, Missouri, from the hands of their enemies.

However, as it turned out, the purposes of Zion's Camp had more to do with the redemption of souls than the redemption of property. Following the long and hot summer journey from Ohio to western Missouri, and after traveling to the doorstep of Jackson County, the Lord revealed, "It is expedient in me that they should be brought thus far *for a trial of their faith*" (D&C 105:19, emphasis added). The Lord knew before He called upon the Saints to raise an army of men to redeem Zion that they were not yet ready to live the laws necessary for her redemption.

Yet, the Lord had a purpose in His command that they travel to Missouri as an army of Saints. Only a relatively few brethren volunteered to journey with Zion's Camp. Before they left their homes in the Eastern states, they recognized that they might lose their lives in battle against the mobs in Missouri. Further, the journey to Missouri itself was a trial of faith that tested their mettle. When cholera broke out among them at the end of the journey, it took the lives of fourteen Saints. The test of these Saints' faith in mortality had been taken and passed. On the February 8, 1835, "the Prophet Joseph Smith called Elders Brigham and Joseph Young to the chamber of his residence, in Kirtland, Ohio, it being on the Sabbath day. . . . He proceeded to relate a vision to these brethren, of the state and condition of those men who died in Zion's Camp, in Missouri. He said, 'Brethren, I have seen those men who died of the cholera in our camp; and the Lord knows, if I get a mansion as bright as theirs, I ask no more.' At this relation he wept, and for some time could not speak."[59] Earlier, the Lord revealed, "I will try you and prove you herewith. And whoso layeth down his life in my cause, for my name's sake, shall find it again, even life eternal. Therefore, be not afraid of your enemies, for I have decreed in my heart, saith the Lord, that I will prove you in all things, whether you will abide in my covenant, even unto death, that you may be found worthy. For if ye will not abide in my covenant ye are not worthy of me" (D&C 98:12–15). Ironically these men gained eternal life through their willingness to lay down their mortal life. Indeed, the plan of salvation rests on this truth—for the very Son of God needed to sacrifice His mortal life to bring to pass immortality and eternal life for all.

This same principle may be applied a thousand times to a thousand other similar circumstances that have and will exist in the tribulations of the last days. Faith in God is strengthened through enduring well in adversity and suffering. President Henry B. Eyring, while talking to students at BYU, related the educating trial of faith his father received before dying of cancer:

> Let me illustrate for you what I know about the questions
> that matter and how they are answered by telling you
> about the last conversations I had with my father. He was
> suffering through the end of a long struggle with bone
> cancer. He still weighed enough and was in such pain that
> it was hard to move him from a chair to his bed. Others far
> more heroic than I spent the months and the days caring
> for him. But I took some turns on the midnight-to-dawn
> shift. . . . One night when I was not with him and the
> pain seemed more than he could bear, he somehow got
> out of bed and on his knees beside it—I know not how.
> He pled with God to know why he was suffering so. And
> the next morning he said, with quiet firmness, "I know
> why now. God needs brave sons."[60]

Elder Eyring's father found meaning in the sufferings that attended his death. I judge that his trust and faith in God was tested and then increased in his ordeal of pain. The aforementioned Zion's Camp afforded the same opportunity. Because of the tribulations, a few of its members became very critical of the Prophet Joseph Smith and left the faith, but others found great spiritual strength in the experience and went on to become significant leaders in the Church. We might say that every individual is sent to earth on a type of Zion's Camp experience. That is, they find themselves in situations in which the purposes are not always clearly understood. The test of faith is how one responds to such situations of mortality.

Along with those involved in Zion's Camp, the ultimate mortal test of faith for all of us may well be death itself, including those last events that lead up to it. It makes no difference what spiritual light one is given in mortality; whether it be the dim, newly rising morning sun or the full resplendent noonday sun, all must die. Job, a towering scriptural example of faith in God, declared his ultimate certainty of divine purpose in the midst of his trials. "Though [the Lord] slay me," he passionately declared, "yet will I trust in him" (Job 13:15)!

Many of the tribulations of the last days will bring death. Many individuals will die, and many will see loved ones die. God did not ordain death to bring misery upon His children. Rather, He designed mortality to draw us closer to Him and to teach us to trust His eternal plan. Death is part of the divine design to end our mortal probation and opens the door for labors in the spirit world and eventual resurrection.

Opportunities Lost to Tribulations and Wickedness

Nothing lost due to the tribulations and wickedness of the last days will truly be lost in the eternities. The Lord's plan provides a period of one thousand years in which losses incurred in mortality may be made up. This period, known as the Millennium, is an essential element of the plan of salvation. Elder Dallin H. Oaks explained:

> Singleness, childlessness, death, and divorce frustrate ideals and postpone the fulfillment of promised blessings. . . . But these frustrations are temporary. The Lord has promised that in the eternities no blessing will be denied his sons and daughters who keep the commandments, are true to their covenants, and desire what is right. Many of the most important deprivations of mortality will be set right in the Millennium, which is the time for fulfilling all that is incomplete in the great plan of happiness for all of our Father's worthy children. We know that will be true of temple ordinances. I believe it will also be true of family relationships and experiences.[61]

Therefore, God's forethought and foreknowledge overcome much of the apparent frustration with His plan. Referring to the Second Coming of the Lord, the Prophet Joseph Smith explained, "At that time the hearts of the widows and fatherless shall be comforted, and every tear shall be wiped from their faces. The trials they have passed through shall work together for their good, and prepare them for the society of those who have come up out of great tribulation, and have washed their robes and made them white in the blood of the lamb."[62]

Thus, we see that no interference of iniquity or physical weakness can prevent the Lord from fulfilling His promises. No disaster or tribulation is too great for Him to overcome.

God Rules over Earthquakes, Disease, and Death

God has declared that as the Creator of the earth, He is the Author of conditions and events of natural disasters, such as earthquakes, hurricanes, famines, and pestilences (see D&C 43:25; 87:6). President Joseph F. Smith explained that we

> believe that God rules in the fire, the earthquake, the tidal wave, the volcanic eruption, and the storm. Him [we]

recognize as the Master and Ruler of nature and her laws, and freely acknowledge his hand in all things. We believe that his judgments are poured out to bring mankind to a sense of his power and his purposes, that they may repent of their sins and prepare themselves for the second coming of Christ to reign in righteousness upon the earth. . . .

We believe that these severe, natural calamities are visited upon men by the Lord for the good of his children, to quicken their devotion to others, and to bring out their better natures, that they may love and serve him. . . .

If these lessons are impressed upon us and upon the people of our country, the anguish, and the loss of life and toil, sad, great and horrifying as they were, will not have been endured in vain.[63]

Although there may be notable exceptions, both the wicked *and* the righteous are exposed to these tribulations in the last days. Earthquakes make no distinction between young and old, male and female, or rich and poor. Children are often the first to die in pestilence and famine. For those who question why God does not regularly intervene to deliver the young from diseases or the righteous from hurricanes, I have asked myself, "What blessing comes from death being unpredictable?" The Lord's purposes for mortality are fulfilled in the irregularity of death. That divine determination provides reason to live each day walking in the paths of righteousness. The unpredictability and randomness of death or debilitating diseases and incapacitating natural events actually increases the importance of our daily acts and choices and erases the attraction of the devilish doctrine of procrastination.

War and Human-Inflicted Suffering

Conditions in the last days seem to portray a world in which the wicked have free reign to carry out their most diabolical schemes. War is poured out on all nations, and armies clash at Armageddon. The destruction of life and challenges of the last days, whether of the Latter-day Saints, the Jews, or any other people, is of such enormity that a note or two more may be appropriate.

First, the Lord is aware, before they transpire, of tribulations that come upon His children and knows everything will work out in His own time. Indeed, we might note that God could have intervened at the height of the

Saints' tribulations in Missouri or in the horrifying unfolding of the Jewish Holocaust. Certainly, many called upon the Messiah to come at those times. However, God revealed that He has determined another timetable for Zion's redemption and the Jewish remnant's temporal and spiritual rescue. To the Saints, He declared, "Ye cannot behold with your natural eyes, for the present time, the design of your God concerning those things which shall come hereafter, and the glory which shall follow after much tribulation. For after much tribulation come the blessings. Wherefore the day cometh that ye shall be crowned with much glory; the hour is not yet, but is nigh at hand" (D&C 58:3–4). The Lord's words will not fail. Zion will be redeemed and built up in her glory. Jesus Christ will appear to the Jewish remnant as their Savior.[64] We need to trust in the Lord and await the wisdom of His timing, which He will manifest to the eyes of all the earth.

Another source of insight concerning God's perspective in allowing the wicked to carry out their evil designs for a season is that of the sufferings heaped upon the Savior anciently by wicked individuals in Jerusalem. When He was yet a babe, Christ's parents took Him to the temple, where the aged Simeon found them. This venerable old patriarch spoke by the power of the Holy Ghost in explaining to Christ's mother, Mary, "Behold, this child is set for the fall and rising again of many in Israel. . . . Yea, a spear shall pierce though him to the wounding of thine own soul also; *that the thoughts of many hearts may be revealed*" (JST, Luke 2:34–35; emphasis added). Human-inflicted sufferings heaped upon the innocent reveal the thoughts and intents of the heart. Those who surrender their will to the devil in the last days reveal in their actions the thoughts of their hearts, and God is aware.

It is necessary that agency be preserved for both the righteous and the wicked. Further, it is necessary for the preservation of agency and the schooling of mortality that our choices have real and often natural consequences. How can we learn the value of obedience and doing good if we are protected from the consequences of our own and others' disobedience and wickedness?

Permitting evil does not suggest that God would have His children choose evil. God's foreknowledge of the wickedness of the last days is not the same as foreordaining that wickedness. During an intimate and revealing experience with God, Enoch saw the Lord weep over the wickedness of the people. When asked, "How is it that thou canst weep, seeing thou art holy, and from all eternity to all eternity?" the Lord explained:

Behold these thy brethren: they are the workmanship of mine own hands, and I gave unto them their knowledge, in the day I created them; and in the Garden of Eden, gave I unto man his agency; and unto thy brethren have I said, and also given commandment, that they should love one another, and that they should choose me, their Father; but behold, they are without affection, and they hate their own blood. . . . Satan shall be their father, and misery their doom; and the whole heavens shall weep over them, even the workmanship of mine hands; wherefore should not the heavens weep, seeing these shall suffer? (Moses 7:29, 32–33, 37)

Thus, in protecting every individual's ability to choose, God weeps with us as He views the sufferings caused by wickedness. However, it appears that His weeping is not only for the suffering of the victims but also for those who inflict such suffering on others. The greater sorrow comes from the fact that anyone would so harden their hearts and choose such terrible wickedness, even if it is in the temporary setting of mortality.

The Lord's Justice for the Wicked

The Lord generally does not use mortality to visibly and fully intervene to bring justice to the wicked. The Lord taught that the wheat and the tares are allowed to grow together until the harvest (see Matthew 13:24–30; D&C 86:1–7). That is, the righteous and the wicked remain in the same world and perform similar tasks during mortality. Further, the Savior emphasized that during this life, God "maketh his sun to rise on the evil and on the good, and sendeth rain on the just and on the unjust" (Matthew 5:45).

Nevertheless, there are appointed times of divine judgment, with accompanying rewards and punishments. None of the wicked are granted immunity from death, whether it comes quickly following their wicked actions or at some later time. In some measure, through death, God intervenes in each wicked individual's life, preventing them from inflicting further wounds. All who live on earth know the day will come when they will take one final breath and pass from this sphere of existence to the next, and it is in that next sphere that God executes justice upon those who inflict evil upon others.

Explaining the distinction between the righteous and the wicked who die and take up their abode in the spirit world, Alma declared,

"Then shall it come to pass that the spirits of the wicked, yea, who are evil—for behold, they have no part nor portion of the Spirit of the Lord; for behold, they chose evil works rather than good; therefore the spirit of the devil did enter into them, and take possession of their house—and these shall be cast out into outer darkness; there shall be weeping, and wailing, and gnashing of teeth, and this because of their own iniquity, being led captive by the will of the devil" (Alma 40:13). "Their torment is as a lake of fire and brimstone, whose flame ascendeth up forever and ever and has no end" (2 Nephi 9:16) or "*endless torment*" (D&C 19:6; emphasis added).

God knew about and organized each aspect of the plan of salvation before the earth was created. The Prophet Joseph Smith taught:

> The great Jehovah contemplated the whole of the events connected with the earth, pertaining to the plan of salvation, before it rolled into existence, or ever "the morning stars sang together" for joy; the past, the present, and the future were and are, with Him, one eternal "now"; He knew of the fall of Adam, the iniquities of the antediluvians, of the depth of iniquity that would be connected with the human family, their weakness and strength, their power and glory, apostasies, their crimes, their righteousness and iniquity; He comprehended the fall of man, and his redemption; He knew the plan of salvation and pointed it out; He was acquainted with the situation of all nations and with their destiny; He ordered all things according to the council of His own will; He knows the situation of both the living and the dead, and has made ample provision for their redemption, according to their several circumstances, and the laws of the kingdom of God, whether in this world, or in the world to come.[65]

The Lord's Justice for the Righteous

The Lord has revealed that the results of wicked individuals' acts, as well as suffering in sickness and death, will not prevail. Regarding the innocent victims of mortality's capriciousness, John the Revelator, while on the Isle of Patmos, heard the heavenly voice declare, "And God shall wipe away all tears from their eyes; and there shall be no more death, neither sorrow, nor crying, neither shall there be any more pain" (Revelation 21:4).

Part of God's intervention at mortal death is that, contrary to the suffering of the wicked, "the spirits of those who are righteous are received into a state of happiness, which is called paradise, a state of rest, a state of peace, where they rest from all their troubles and from all care, and sorrow" (Alma 40:12). It follows that they are placed beyond the clutches of the designing and evil individuals who tormented them in mortality and beyond the challenges of a corruptible world. Spirits are placed beyond the reach of pain, suffering, hunger, and death. Mortal riches no longer have any meaning for thieves to afflict the innocent. Because the dead do not have bodies of flesh and bone in the spirit world, a host of physical maladies no longer afflict their persons. The righteous are free from suffering.

In the case of both the wicked and the righteous, the Atonement must take effect. While the effect on the righteous is immediate and they are caught up in rest and paradise, the effect on the wicked takes time. They are left to suffer for their iniquities until they are taught about the mercies of the Atonement, its attendant requirements, and the ordinances of salvation. Ironically, it may be the very victims of evil deeds who later serve as missionaries to preach to the wicked spirits in prison.

Although God's intervention is postponed, the deferment is designed in perfect wisdom for all involved. The righteous lose nothing in the eternal perspective but gain everything that may have been taken from them in mortality, and furthermore, they will receive all of the blessings God can bestow upon them for their strength of character, each according to their individual choices and the degree of their faithfulness. At the appropriate time, their joy will increase when their spirits are inseparably united with their resurrected bodies and they are "brought to stand before God, and be judged according to their works" (Alma 40:21). Thus, although the Lord's retribution for wickedness and blessings for righteousness are sure, they are not premature. "A premature showing of His power and strength in support of His Saints," Elder Neal A. Maxwell explained, "could cut short the trial of our faith."[66]

Yet, the time will come, as promised, "that Satan shall have no more power over the hearts of the children of men; for the day soon cometh that all the proud and they who do wickedly shall be as stubble; and the day cometh that they must be burned. For the time soon cometh that the fulness of the wrath of God shall be poured out upon all the children of men; for he will not suffer that the wicked shall destroy the righteous. . . . Wherefore, the righteous need not fear" (1 Nephi 22:15–17). "For in mine own due time will I come upon the earth in judgment," the Savior promised, "and my people shall be redeemed and shall reign with me on the earth. For the great Millennium, of which I have spoken by the mouths of my servants, shall come" (D&C 43: 29–30).

6

RIGHTEOUSNESS SHALL SWEEP THE EARTH

LIGHT AND TRUTH TRIUMPH OVER darkness and cunning. God's power and people will prevail over evil in bringing forth Zion. The last days surely include times of great challenges, but they also embrace the greatest epoch on earth since its creation. The Lord promised in the last days, "I will pour out my spirit upon all flesh" (Joel 2:28). This outpouring of God's Spirit extends to all: sons, daughters, old men, young men, servants, and handmaids (Joel 2:28–29). As a result, minds are enlightened with understanding and hearts are enlivened with hope. The Lord vowed that in the last days, "righteousness and truth will I cause to sweep the earth as with a flood" (Moses 7:62).

The Lord never intended to permit iniquity to abound without countering Satan's influence with the fulness of the priesthood and the Restoration of the gospel. Indeed, God foreordained that in the last days there would be greater light in contrast to the darkness that will seek to cover the earth. Tribulations may descend, but God's work will go forward. In response to Martin Harris breaking his covenant and losing the first 116 manuscript pages of the Book of Mormon translation, the Savior declared, "The works, and the designs, and the purposes of God cannot be frustrated, neither can they come to naught" (D&C 3:1). Among His many purposes, Christ has restored His Church, His authority, and His true doctrine.

Prelude to the Restoration

The Restoration was built upon the labors of those God inspired centuries earlier. These earlier lights guided others to the truth and provided needed progress toward the dawning of a new day. Some individuals received inspiration in the realm of the spiritual, while others were enlightened to bless the world with technological advances. For example, before the Book of Mormon could be published and sent to the world, the days of scribal monks copying texts by hand needed to give way to the printing press. Likewise, for the Book of Mormon to fulfill its mission as a second witness of the resurrected Jesus Christ, the Bible needed to flood the earth ahead of the Nephite record. Thus, the invention of the moveable-type printing press and Gutenberg's use of it in Germany were an essential precursor to the Restoration of the gospel and, in turn, to Christ's Second Coming. This is equally true of the need for the Bible to be translated from Hebrew, Greek, and Latin into the languages of the common people. The Lord inspired and gave fire to the souls of translators and, subsequently, to Christian missionaries who traveled to the far reaches of the globe, blessing humanity with the message and testimony of the Bible.

Those living in the last days benefit from other significant events that prepared the way for the Restoration of the gospel and eventually for taking that message and the Church of Jesus Christ to all the world.[67] Among these other significant events and movements was the Renaissance and its influence on religious reform in Europe. The Protestant Reformation was a type of pre-Restoration. The work and teachings of individuals such as Martin Luther, Ulrich Zwingli, and John Calvin paved the way for religious thought outside of the Catholic tradition. The Anabaptists emphasized the need for believer baptism in contrast to infant baptism and sought a complete separation of church and state. "Emphasis was given to righteous living," LDS historian De Lamar Jensen wrote, "and to following the precepts taught by Jesus Christ. . . . other reformers placed more emphasis on behavior than on doctrine and more reliance on human will than on human depravity."[68]

Other pre-Restoration events were of at least equal importance: Christopher Columbus sailing to the Americas, European origins of liberty, the rise of a free nation in America, and contributions of specific nations, such as Great Britain and France, as champions of human liberties in the modern world. The establishment of the United States is a major contribution in preparing the way for the seeds of the gospel to be planted and to flourish. In the early stages, this latter-day nation provided a base for early missionaries to take the message of the Restoration across borders and oceans and to be joined by converts in taking the gospel to the entire world. The Lord showed Nephi that the Restoration of the gospel was built upon the foundation of these and other important events (see 1 Nephi 13–14).

As part of the preparation for the Restoration of the gospel, the Lord has and will continue to pour out His Spirit upon the earth to provide the necessary technology for accomplishing His work. "From the day that He and His Beloved Son manifested themselves to the boy Joseph," President Gordon B. Hinckley declared,

> There has been a tremendous cascade of enlightenment poured out upon the world. . . . The vision of Joel has been fulfilled wherein he declared: "And it shall come to pass afterward, that I will pour out my spirit upon all flesh; and your sons and your daughters shall prophesy, your old men shall dream dreams, your young men shall see visions: And also upon the servants and upon the handmaids in those days will I pour out my spirit" (Joel 2:28–29). . . .
>
> There has been more of scientific discovery during these years than during all of the previous history of mankind. Transportation, communication, medicine, public hygiene, the unlocking of the atom, the miracle of the computer, with all of its ramifications, have blossomed forth, particularly in our own era. During my own lifetime, I have witnessed miracle after wondrous miracle come to pass. We take it for granted.[69]

The Restoration of the Gospel: A Great Sign of the Last Days

The ushering in of the dispensation of the fulness of times is the greatest single sign of the last days. Every other event and advancement pales in significance to the bright splendor of the Lord's work in restoring the fulness of His gospel to the earth again. The shadows of past apostasy faded in the light of the truth that came from heaven. The First Vision was the most important latter-day event; it announced the beginning of the last days and the nearness of the Second Coming. The Restoration of truth did not occur overnight. When God the Father and Jesus Christ appeared to Joseph, the Savior promised the Prophet Joseph Smith "that the true doctrine—the fulness of the gospel—should, at some future time, be made known to him."[70] The angel Moroni tutored the young Joseph for four years before he entrusted Joseph with the Book of Mormon plates. Each year on September 21–22, the two met on the Hill Cumorah. Joseph recorded that he "received instruction and intelligence from him at each of our interviews, respecting what the Lord was going to do, and how and in what manner his kingdom was to be conducted *in the last days*" (Joseph Smith—History 1:54; emphasis added). Moroni further informed Joseph "that the preparatory work for the second coming of the Messiah was speedily to commence; that the time was at hand for the Gospel, in all its fulness to be preached in power, unto all nations that a people might be prepared for the Millennial reign."[71]

Old Testament prophets, such as Moses, Isaiah, Jeremiah, and Ezekiel, foretold that in the last days the Lord would again gather scattered Israel.[72] This gathering was prophesied to occur in the last days when the Lord would again establish Zion. Further through Isaiah, the Lord exhorted latter-day Israel to "put on thy strength, O Zion" (Isaiah 52:1). The Prophet Joseph Smith explained that in this exhortation, the Lord promised that in the last days the remnants of Israel would once more "hold the power of priesthood to bring again Zion, and the redemption of Israel" (D&C 113:8). As the essential precursor to the restoration of Israel, the risen Lord taught the Nephites that the coming forth of the Book of Mormon was "a sign, that ye may know the time when these things [the prophesied latter-day gathering of Israel] shall be about to take place" (3 Nephi 21:1).

The restoration of the Aaronic and Melchizedek priesthoods in 1829 led to thousands and millions of missionaries going forth to the inhabitants of the earth and "the scattered remnants [being] exhorted to return to the Lord from whence they have fallen" (D&C 113:10)— commencing the gathering of Israel. The gathering fulfills the prophecy given through the prophet Jeremiah concerning the last days:

> Therefore, behold, the days come, saith the Lord, that it shall no more be said, The Lord liveth, that brought up the children of Israel out of the land of Egypt; but, The Lord liveth, that brought up the children of Israel from the land of the north, and from all the lands whither he had driven them: and I will bring them again into their land that I gave unto their fathers. Behold, I will send for many fishers, saith the Lord, and they shall fish them; and after will I send for many hunters, and they shall hunt them from every mountain, and from every hill, and out of the holes of the rocks. (Jeremiah 16:14–16)

Preach the Gospel as a Witness to All Nations

The Lord not only promised to gather Israel in the last days, but He also foretold that before He returns, He will give a witness of the Restoration to all nations. Like the Restoration itself, the ability of missionaries to bear witness to all nations has benefitted greatly from concurrent progress in the technology of the last days. The missionary message that the fulness of the gospel has been restored to the earth has gone forth at an ever-increasing pace.

A moment of review may help the reader ponder and better envision this sign of the last days and how it has and is being fulfilled. In 1830, Samuel Smith, the first missionary of the newly organized Church of Jesus Christ, left the Palmyra, New York, area with a knapsack on his back, filled with copies of the newly published Book of Mormon. He walked to nearby towns to share his testimony of the Restoration. Other missionaries followed in his footsteps and then boarded brightly painted packet boats on the Erie Canal. The canal was an amazing vehicle that connected with other transportation marvels of the age—the railroad car and the steamboat—providing means to journey from Buffalo to New York City. Towns all along their path were open to missionaries. Huge ships capable of making the transatlantic voyage sailed from New York City, taking missionaries to Great Britain, Ireland, Scandinavia, the European continent, and beyond. As decades quickly passed, missionaries were able to take the message of the Restoration to all the corners of the world by means of railroads, paved interstate roads, and, eventually, jumbo jet airplanes. Missionaries contacted individuals and families at homes, in the market, and through World's Fair pavilions.

Copies of the Book of Mormon first came from individual lead-letter pieces of type tediously set by hand for printing. After the type had been set, each sheet was printed on an Acorn Hand Press and hung to dry, after which the collective pages were taken to the bindery. Eventually, E. B. Grandin's press and print shop, with the help of a new press, put out five thousand copies of the Book of Mormon. As marvelous as this new modern press was, it was soon replaced by newer and more efficient presses. The earth was being flooded with copies of the Book of Mormon that testified that Jesus is the Christ. Today, the Book of Mormon, Bible, Doctrine and Covenants, and Pearl of Great Price rapidly fly from high-speed presses that challenge the human eye to catch them in their work. Additionally, digitally written and audio copies of the scriptures and other Church materials are downloaded daily to home computers and handheld devices.

Pageants proclaiming the Restoration have graced hillsides with audiences in the hundreds of thousands. Well-written and well-directed video productions tell the story of the Restoration and share testimonies of members with all who will listen. Music, the spoken word, dance, drama, and blog spots proclaim the glorious blessings of Christ's gospel and Church.

In the 1830s, friends and family wrote letters to their loved ones sharing their joy and testimony of the restored gospel. Today, electronic messages via the Internet join weariless mail carriers in spreading the good news. Telephones and video cams on computers link people together and provide additional means of communication between those who know the gospel and those who wish to know it. My youngest son communicates weekly face-to-face via his video cam on an iPad with individuals he met as a missionary in Ukraine. Messages of prophets and apostles have been broadcast over radio, then television, followed by satellite and Internet to the far reaches of the globe. Missionary training centers have been set up in many countries to prepare young and old to serve as capable ambassadors of Christ and His Church, to help them learn foreign languages and acquire skills to better communicate the greatest message since angels declared the Resurrection of the Son of God in the meridian of time.

Most significantly, the Lord promised His servants, "I have kept in store a blessing such as is not known among the children of men, and it shall be poured forth upon their heads. And from thence men shall go forth into all nations" (D&C 39:15). This blessing was first given to those who gathered to Kirtland, Ohio. The early Saints built a temple in which they could be "endowed with power from on high" (D&C 38:32). Further, the Lord promised them, "I will go before your face. I will be on your right hand and on your left, and my Spirit shall be in your hearts, and mine angels round about you, to bear you up" (D&C 84:88). At the dedication of the Kirtland Temple, the Prophet Joseph Smith prayed: "And we ask thee, Holy Father, that thy servants may go forth from this house armed with thy power, and that thy name may be upon them, and thy glory be round about them, and thine angels have charge over them; and from this place they may bear exceedingly great and glorious tidings, in truth, unto the ends of the earth, that they may know that this is thy work, and that thou hast put forth thy hand, to fulfill that which thou hast spoken by the mouths of the prophets, concerning the last days" (D&C 109:22–23). The work of preaching the gospel to all the world has gone forth since the early days of the Restoration, declared by those that have been endowed in the houses of the Lord. The Spirit of God that attends the teaching of the gospel is more powerful than all of the glorious technological advances with which we have been blessed. Thousands of missionaries study the scriptures to first obtain the word of God, and then as they are worthy and seek the Spirit of God, it is poured out upon them, fulfilling the Lord's promise, "You shall have my Spirit and my word, yea, the power of God unto the convincing of men" (D&C 11:21).

All of these labors combine in the Saints' efforts to fulfill the Savior's command that "the word may go forth unto the ends of the earth. . . . For it shall come to pass in that day, that every man shall hear the fulness of the gospel in his own tongue, and in his own language, through those who are ordained unto this power" (D&C 90:9, 11).

Never before has the Church of Jesus Christ been established in every nation and among every kindred and people. This destiny was made clear more than two thousand five hundred years ago when Daniel interpreted Babylonian King Nebuchadnezzar's dream. Following an age of empires and kingdoms in Asia and Europe, "shall the God of heaven set up a kingdom," Daniel explained, "which shall never be destroyed: and the kingdom shall not be left to other people, but it shall break in pieces and consume all these kingdoms, and it shall stand forever" (Daniel 2:44). In preparation for the day when the Lord would return to receive this kingdom and reign over the earth, the Lord explained that "the keys of the kingdom of God are committed unto man on the earth, and from thence shall the gospel roll forth unto the ends of the earth, as the stone which is cut out of the mountain without hands shall roll forth, until it has filled the whole earth" (D&C 65:2). "It is no light thing for any people in any age of the world to have a dispensation of the Gospel of Jesus Christ committed into their hands," Wilford Woodruff taught, "and when a dispensation has been given, those receiving it are held responsible before high heaven for the use they make of it."[73]

Without the Restoration of the fulness of the gospel on the earth prior to Christ's return, "the whole earth would be utterly wasted at his coming" (D&C 2:3).[74] What conditions should exist in the kingdom of God at the time of the Savior's return to receive that kingdom? As discussed earlier, the Lord revealed to the prophet Enoch His plan for establishing His kingdom preparatory to His return. "Righteousness will I send down out of heaven," God declared, "and truth will I send forth out of the earth, to bear testimony of mine Only Begotten; his resurrection from the dead; yea, and also the resurrection of all men" (Moses 7:62). President Ezra Taft Benson explained:

> The Lord promised, therefore, that righteousness would come from heaven and truth out of the earth. We have seen the marvelous fulfillment of that prophecy in our generation. The Book of Mormon has come forth out of the earth, filled with truth, serving as the very "keystone of our religion" (see Introduction to the Book of Mormon). God has also sent down righteousness from heaven. The Father Himself appeared with His Son to the Prophet Joseph Smith. The angel Moroni, John the Baptist, Peter, James, and numerous other angels were directed by heaven to restore the necessary powers to the kingdom. Further, the Prophet Joseph Smith received revelation after revelation from the heavens during those first critical years of the Church's growth. These revelations have been preserved for us in the Doctrine and Covenants.[75]

If we only paint the prophesied iniquity and tribulations of the last days on our canvas of understanding, much of the picture will be missing. The earth must be cleansed of wickedness, *and* righteousness must be established to prepare for the Lord's return and the Millennium. As the continued explanation of that righteousness, which is part of the last days, the Lord revealed to Enoch, "Righteousness and truth will I cause to sweep the earth as with a flood, to gather out mine elect from the four quarters of the earth" (Moses 7:62). The iniquity of the last days is countered by the righteousness of God's kingdom. The good of all nations have refuge from the storm in the stakes of Zion. Like a great flood, the power of virtue and the strength of truth moves forward, gathering the righteous to the Church of Jesus Christ.

In summary of the message of the Restoration of the gospel going forth to all the world in the last days, the Prophet Joseph Smith wrote, "The Standard of Truth has been erected; no unhallowed hand can stop the work from progressing; persecutions may rage, mobs may combine, armies may assemble, calumny may defame, but the truth of God will go forth boldly, nobly, and independent, till it has penetrated every continent, visited every clime, swept every country, and sounded in every ear, till the purposes of God shall be accomplished, and the Great Jehovah shall say the work is done."76

7
PREPARATION FOR
THE SECOND COMING

THE LORD'S GUIDANCE OF HOW we are to live in the last days and how to prepare for the Second Coming is at least as important as knowing the signs of His coming. When I was a young boy, I had a very vivid dream that still remains with me fifty or so years later. In my dream, it was a summer day, and I had eagerly awoken and made the trek up the stairs from my bedroom in our basement. I went to our living room and opened the front door to our home. Our home faced the majestic mountains east of Salt Lake Valley. I anticipated seeing the sun come up over the mountaintops as I had so many other mornings. To my surprise, the light of the sun did not rise, but rather the light came from the Savior coming over the tops of the mountains with hosts of angels. I felt an indescribable fear that I was not ready for this event to occur so soon in my life. My response was to quickly close our front door, hoping that this action might give me a little more time to prepare for the Second Coming. I do not recall the particular sins for which I felt I needed to repent. But I do remember that I felt my young life was not what it should have been. How does one prepare for the Savior's return? What can we do to rejoice in the Second Coming rather than feel that we would like to hide or have more time to get ready?

Preparation for the Second Coming includes successfully navigating the iniquity and tribulations of the last days. The foundation for righteously preparing begins on the individual level and extends to our family, community, Church, and world efforts.

Individual Spiritual Preparation

"We need to make both temporal and spiritual preparation for the events prophesied at the time of the Second Coming," Elder Dallin H. Oaks advised. "And the preparation most likely to be neglected is the one less visible and more difficult—the spiritual. A 72-hour kit of temporal supplies may prove valuable for earthly challenges, but, as the foolish virgins learned to their sorrow, a 24-hour kit of spiritual preparation is of greater and more enduring value."[77]

The most predominant scriptural theme for preparing for the Second Coming is the same as the theme for preparing to meet God in any age or dispensation of the world—individual righteousness. I believe that one of the best discourses to serve as a means to conduct a self-searching interview is found in the Prophet Alma's questions to the people in Zarahemla. A brief review of his discourse is very insightful.

Alma's first questions deal with remembrance. One of the means by which we can be better prepared spiritually is to remember—specifically, to remember the testimonies and faith of those who have gone before us. The Lord delivered Alma's father and the members of the Church in that day from Lamanite bondage. More important, previous to that bondage, they were under the bondage of sin during the reign of the wicked King Noah. The Lord sent the prophet Abinadi to call them to repentance. Alma reminded them that their fathers were delivered from spiritual bondage through faith in Abinadi's testimony of the Son of God. "Did not my father Alma believe in the words which were delivered by the mouth of Abinadi?" Alma the Younger asked. "And according to his faith there was a mighty change wrought in his heart," he continued. "And behold, he preached the word unto your fathers, and a mighty change was also wrought in their hearts, and they humbled themselves and put their trust in the true and living God. And behold, they were faithful until the end; therefore they were saved" (Alma 5:11–13).

Alma proceeded to ask those in Zarahemla a series of questions each of us can answer in our own personal preparation for the Second Coming:

> Have ye spiritually been born of God? Have ye received his image in your countenances? Have ye experienced this mighty change in your hearts?
>
> Do ye exercise faith in the redemption of him who created you? Do you look forward with an eye of faith, and view this mortal body raised in immortality . . . to stand before God to be judged according to the deeds which have been done in the mortal body? . . .
>
> Can you imagine to yourselves that ye hear the voice of the Lord, saying unto you, in that day: Come unto me

ye blessed, for behold, your works have been the works of
righteousness upon the face of the earth? . . .

Can ye look up to God at that day with a pure heart
and clean hands? (Alma 5:14–16, 19)

I will leave it to you, the reader, to study the remainder of the self-
interrogation suggestions Alma gave his people. Each individual will
meet God, whether they live to see the Savior come in the clouds of
heaven or die before that time and hope to return with Him.

I have tasted a bit of what I hope will be true regarding my future
in relation to the Lord's return to the earth. I have had the incredible
opportunity of living in Jerusalem with my family while teaching at the
Brigham Young University Jerusalem Center for Near Eastern Studies.
One of the greatest blessings that experience offered was to have constant
reminders of the Savior's mortal life. Another was that each morning I
looked out on the sunlight illuminating the Old City and especially the
Temple Mount. I had many opportunities to reflect on the events of
Gethsemane, Golgotha, and the Garden Tomb.

Among all of these memories, one stands out in relation to a study
of the last days and the Second Coming. I spent many hours on the
Mount of Olives, individually and with my family and students. I
imagined what it might be to witness the Savior descend upon that
mount in His appearance to the Jewish remnant. In my mind's eye, I
saw their faces as He showed them the wounds in His hands and feet. I
envisioned the tears of joy and sadness in their eyes to have their Messiah
return to save them from their enemies. The question I asked myself is,
where might I be at that monumental moment? I mused that I would
be to the north of the Savior, on my patio outside our apartment at the
Jerusalem Center, watching the glorious happenings from a distance. The
Savior would turn to His new Jewish believers and declare, "I wish for
you to learn my gospel and to receive the ordinances of salvation." Then
pointing to me, He would ask, "Do you see that man standing on his
patio? That is Craig Ostler. He is my disciple. He will teach and guide you
in the paths of righteousness that will bring you into my kingdom that
you may be one with me."

I believe much good can come from envisioning our personal state
and preparation at the Second Coming. Where will you be? What will
you be found doing? I do not really expect that I'll be in Jerusalem at
that moment or that you will be there either. But wherever we might be,
the most important questions to answer will be, have we had a mighty

change of heart? Have we been faithful disciples of Christ? Are we individuals He can trust to teach others how to live His gospel?

Preparation for Jesus Christ's Second Coming Is Similar to Preparation for His First Coming

Another way of thinking about preparation for the Second Coming is to compare your state to those who were prepared for the Savior's first coming. Those who were prepared to recognize and receive the Savior in the meridian of time were willing to repent of their sins. John the Baptist prepared many of them and taught them to bring forth fruits of repentance, covenant with God in the waters of baptism, and live the commandments. In addition, many had searched the scriptures to become familiar with the prophecies that would attend the Messiah and were able to see fulfillment of those prophesies as they occurred or as they reflected on past events. Most importantly, those who received Jesus of Nazareth as the Christ accepted the Holy Spirit for their guide and trusted in the impressions they received. Among those who recognized Jesus as the Christ when He was no more than a babe or a child were Elizabeth, Joseph, Mary, Simeon, Anna, the Magi, and the shepherds in the fields near Bethlehem. When Jesus began His ministry, to this number were added myriads of others, including Peter, Peter's brother Andrew, Jesus' brothers James and John, Mary Magdalene, and Lazarus and his sisters, Mary and Martha. When the story of the last days is written for millennial-day Saints to read, it would be incredible to be included in the accounts of those who were the Savior's faithful disciples in the last days.

The claim is often made that the reason the Jews who lived during the Savior's mortal life did not recognize Him is that they confused the prophecies of His Second Coming with the prophecies of His mortal birth and ministry. Likewise, it appears that one of the reasons those who study scriptures in the last days may fail to recognize the signs of the Savior's return is that they confuse which events are actually associated with the Second Coming with those that precede it or follow it. In addition, some may confuse the specific events regarding His appearance to the Jewish remnant upon the Mount of Olives with signs of His appearances in Adam-ondi-Ahman, Jackson County, and to the world.

While teaching His disciples on the Mount of Olives, the Savior twice emphasized the need to avoid deception in the last days. He also gave two means of overcoming that deception. First, He referred to the importance of the Holy Ghost for those who "are wise and have received the truth, and have taken the Holy Spirit for their guide, and have not been deceived" (D&C 45:57). Second, He promised, "Whoso treasureth up my word, shall not be deceived" (Joseph Smith—Matthew 1:37). A correct knowledge and understanding of the scriptures and how they apply to us may serve as "the shield of faith wherewith ye shall be able to quench all the fiery darts of the wicked" (D&C 27:17).

Avoid Despair

For nearly two hundred years, members of the Church of Jesus Christ have hoped for and anticipated that Christ would return during their lifetime. Unwise worry concerning the calamities foretold does nothing more than bring confusion and distress. The Lord indicated that those who are prepared will not fear (D&C 38:30).

The gospel gives us hope for the present and hope that extends beyond this life. Tribulations are part of mortality, and "he that is faithful in tribulation, the reward of the same is greater in the kingdom of heaven" (D&C 58:2). It may be more difficult to live in the last days and to fulfill the purposes of mortality, but the Lord knows our abilities. Some individuals actually seem to do better when life is harder. Trials sharpen their focus and inspire them to greater righteousness.

Youth may need encouragement to maintain a positive outlook on the future. President Boyd K. Packer reflected on his fears as a young man. "Sometimes you might be tempted to think as I did from time to time in my youth," Elder Packer shared. "'The way things are going, the world's going to be over with. The end of the world is going to come before I get to where I should be.' Not so! You can look forward to doing it right—getting married, having a family, seeing your children and grandchildren, maybe even great-grandchildren."[78] Clearly, we should not allow fears of the last days to cause us to despair of setting goals for life. Actually, the truth is quite the opposite. The events of the signs of the times may offer greater opportunities to get to where you should be. Regardless of when the Savior returns, the Second Coming will usher in the Millennium, at which time the earth will be given for an inheritance to those who have taken the Holy Spirit as their guide. "And they shall multiply and wax strong, and their children shall grow up without sin unto salvation" (D&C 45:58). Thus, whether the time is so short that one may not marry or raise a family before the Second Coming is really not an issue. Be it before the Savior returns or during the Millennium, the Lord's promises will all be fulfilled for each individual.

Wise Temporal Preparation

A wise person knows to take an umbrella and put on a coat in preparation for a cold, rainy day. In many ways, cold, rainy days have been forecast for the last days. Wisdom counsels that we be prepared for the times of tribulation in which we do and will live. President Gordon B. Hinckley asked, "What we have experienced in the past was all foretold, and the end is not yet. Just as there have been calamities in the past, we expect more in the future. What do we do?" He answered:

> We can so live that we can call upon the Lord for His protection and guidance. This is a first priority. We cannot expect His help if we are unwilling to keep His command-ments. . . .
>
> We can heed warnings. . . .
>
> We have built grain storage and storehouses and stocked them with the necessities of life in the event of a disaster. But the best storehouse is the family storeroom. In words of revelation the Lord has said, "Organize yourselves; prepare every needful thing" (D&C 109:8).
>
> Our people for three-quarters of a century have been counseled and encouraged to make such preparation as will assure survival should a calamity come.
>
> We can set aside some water, basic food, medicine, and clothing to keep us warm. We ought to have a little money laid aside in case of a rainy day.
>
> Now what I have said should not occasion a run on the grocery store or anything of that kind. I am saying nothing that has not been said for a very long time.[79]

Preparation of the Church of Jesus Christ to Meet the Tribulations of the Last Days

The Lord explained, "Wherefore, I the Lord, knowing the calamity which should come upon the inhabitants of the earth, called upon my servant Joseph Smith, Jun., and spake unto him from heaven, and gave him commandments" (D&C 1:17). Christ called on the Prophet Joseph Smith and others to carry out His work in the last days. The Savior's instructions regarding the condition of the kingdom at the time of His coming were encapsulated in three parables. The last of the Savior's three parables regarding preparation for the Second Coming dealt with His "admonition to feed the hungry, give drink to the thirsty, take in the stranger, clothe the naked, and visit the sick and those in prison."[80]

The Lord explained that the command to care for the poor was not to be fully fulfilled one by one. Rather, this endeavor was to be accomplished by the combined consecrated efforts of all of the Saints. To that end, Christ instructed that Church leaders organize themselves to establish a "storehouse for the poor of my people" (D&C 78:3). He informed the Saints that by preparing in this seemingly small way to care for the poor, the time would come in which, "through my providence, notwithstanding the tribulation which shall descend upon you, that the church may stand independent above all other creatures beneath the celestial world" (D&C 78:14). Consequently, Church leaders established a Church-owned company known as the United Firm to oversee the care of the poor, the publishing of church materials, and the building of the New Jerusalem.[81] The members of the United Firm guided the work and made decisions based on the principles revealed in the laws of consecration and stewardship. From the beginning of the United Firm, the Lord made it known that "this order I have appointed to be an everlasting order unto you, and unto your successors" (D&C 82:20). Today, a greatly expanded work of the original United Firm is carried out by the office of the Presiding Bishopric under the direction of the First Presidency of the Church.

Through the decades that have passed since the initial efforts to organize the Church to care for the poor and needy, the ability to fulfill the Lord's commands has continually increased. The original storehouse for the poor was located in a small first-floor room of Newel K. Whitney's store in Kirtland, Ohio. The continual efforts of the Church to provide for the needy are surely a fulfillment of the Lord's admonition, "Wherefore, be not weary in well-doing, for ye are laying the foundation of a great work. And out of small things proceedeth that which is great" (D&C 64:33).

Today the Church's welfare and humanitarian programs reach out to meet the needs of many individuals worldwide. Funds come first from the monthly fast, in which "members of the Church go without food or drink for two consecutive meals and contribute a fast offering at least equal to the value of two meals. Bishops then use the fast offerings to care for those in need."[82] In addition, the Church has established storehouses in many locations, from which, under the direction of bishops, the poor can receive needed commodities, as well as receive training and learn of employment opportunities.

The Church's efforts to reach out to the needy extend across the earth to those who are not members. Those who have more than is needed have opportunity to provide for those who lack. Fellow Saints from ages past have joined in these efforts whenever and wherever they have lived. For example, Alma wrote of the Church in his day: "In their prosperous circumstances, they did not send away any who were naked, or that were hungry, or that were athirst, or that were sick, or that had not been nourished; and they did not set their hearts upon riches; therefore they were liberal to all, both old and young, both bond and free, both male and female, whether out of the church or in the church, having no respect to persons as to those who stood in need" (Alma 1:30).

With each new day, the Church seeks to be better prepared to reach those in need. Those efforts will most likely only increase as the prophesied tribulations of the last days unfold again and again. A love for our fellow beings and faith in God motivate us to sacrifice to provide welfare and humanitarian relief. "From the beginning this Church has moved forward with faith," President Gordon B. Hinckley declared. "Faith was the strength of the Prophet Joseph. . . . And so it has been with each of the Presidents of the Church. In the face of terrible opposition, they have moved forward with faith. . . . More recently, whether it was an urgent need to extend humanitarian aid to victims of the tsunami, or earthquakes, or floods in divers places, it has all been the same. Welfare shelves have been emptied. Cash by the millions has been dispatched to those in need, regardless of Church membership—all in faith."[83]

Whenever and wherever disasters occur, the Church is committed to relieving the victims' suffering. Some years ago, President Hinckley spoke in Managua, Nicaragua, to one thousand, three hundred Church members who had survived a devastating hurricane that claimed more than eleven thousand lives. He said, "As long as the Church has resources, we will not let you go hungry or without clothing or without shelter. We shall do all that we can to assist in the way that the Lord has designated that it should be done."[84]

Temporal care for the needy is closely tied to the spiritual health of the Church. When hundreds of handcart pioneers were stranded in the snow-packed plains of Wyoming, President Brigham Young clarified, "I will tell you all that your faith, religion, and profession of religion, will never save one soul of you in the celestial kingdom of our God, unless you . . . bring in those people now on the plains, and attend strictly to those things which we call temporal, or temporal duties, otherwise your faith will be in vain."[85]

When he was the Presiding Bishop responsible for overseeing the temporal concerns of the Church, H. David Burton explained,

> No matter how many temples we build, no matter how large our membership grows, no matter how positively we are perceived in the eyes of the world—should we fail in this great core commandment to "succor the weak, lift up the hands which hang down, and strengthen the feeble knees," (D&C 81:5) or turn our hearts from those who suffer and mourn, we are under condemnation and cannot please the Lord. . . . Throughout the world, nearly 28,000 bishops search after the poor to administer to their needs. Each bishop is assisted by a ward council consisting of priesthood and auxiliary leaders, including a devoted Relief Society president. They can "fly to the relief of the stranger; . . . pour in oil and wine to the wounded heart of the distressed; . . . [and] dry up the tears of the orphan and make the widow's heart to rejoice" (Joseph Smith, *History of the Church*, 4:567–68).[86]

One of the reasons the Lord restored His Church to the earth in the last days was so He, through His Saints, could alleviate the suffering He knew would attend earthquakes, tsunamis, tempests, pestilences, scourges, and wars. The Church and its members have been blessed to be able to help with needed commodities, such as food, medical supplies, clothing, and hygiene and newborn kits. Opportunities to have the Savior proclaim, "Inasmuch as ye have done it unto one of the least of these my brethren, ye have done it unto me" (Matthew 25:40), will surely abound for all who live in the last days.

Stand Ye in Holy Places: Stakes of Zion

The Savior indicated that in the last days His "disciples shall stand in holy places, and shall not be moved" (D&C 45:32). The previously discussed call to personal righteousness is certainly part of standing in holy places. The Lord revealed that He implied additional meaning when He referred to His Saints gathering "in unto one place upon the face of this land, to prepare their hearts and to be prepared in all things against the day when tribulation and desolation are sent forth upon the wicked" (D&C 29:8). The latter-day gathering the Lord's prophets are directing provides both opportunity and responsibilities to unite with others in preparing for the Savior to return to the earth. In 1831, at the time the Lord revealed anew His Olivet Discourse, He also commanded the newly baptized members of His Church, "With one heart and with one mind, gather up your riches that ye may purchase an inheritance. . . . And it shall be called the New Jerusalem, a land of peace, a city of refuge, a place of safety for the saints of the Most High God. . . . And there shall be gathered unto it out of every nation under heaven" (D&C 45:65–66, 69).

After the Prophet Joseph Smith traveled to the western borders of Missouri in obedience to the Lord's command, he asked, "When will Zion be built up in her glory, and where will thy Temple stand, unto which all nations shall come in the last days?"[87] In answer to his plea, the Lord revealed that the land in and around Jackson County, Missouri, "is the land of promise, and the place for the city of Zion" (D&C 57:2). "Independence," the Lord more specifically designated, "is the center place; and a spot for the temple is lying westward, upon a lot which is not far from the courthouse" (D&C 57:3).

The Saints did not prove worthy to remain in Zion to build the temple. The Savior referred to them as salt that had lost its savor (see D&C 101:1–8, 39–40). Yet, "Zion shall not be moved out of her place, notwithstanding her children are scattered," the Lord affirmed. "They that remain, and are pure in heart, shall return, and come to their inheritances, they and their children, with songs of everlasting joy, to build up the waste places of Zion" (D&C 101:17–18). However, the Lord also revealed, "I have other places which I will appoint unto them, and they shall be called stakes, for the curtains or the strength of Zion. Behold, it is my will, that all they who call on my name . . . should gather together, and *stand in holy places*" (D&C 101:21–22; emphasis added).

Thus, Zion is not limited to one city or land, although the concept of Zion may be understood in its infant state as a city. Isaiah prophesied that Zion "[shall] break forth on the right hand and on the left" (Isaiah

54:3). "You know there has been great discussion in relation to Zion," the Prophet Joseph Smith taught, "where it is, and where the gathering of the dispensation is, and which I am now going to tell you. The prophets have spoken and written upon it; but I will make a proclamation that will cover a broader ground. The whole of America is Zion itself from north to south, and is described by the Prophets, who declare that it is the Zion where the mountain of the Lord should be, and that it should be in the center of the land."[88]

When the early Saints "first heard the fulness of the Gospel preached by the first Elders," Elder Erastus Snow explained, "and read the revelations given through the Prophet Joseph Smith, our ideas of Zion were very limited. But as our minds began to grow and expand, why we began to look upon Zion as a great people, and the Stakes of Zion as numerous. . . . We ceased to set bounds to Zion and her Stakes."[89]

In the dedicatory prayer for the Kirtland temple, the Prophet Joseph Smith petitioned the Lord:

> Prepare the hearts of thy saints for all those judgments thou art about to send, in thy wrath, upon the inhabitants of the earth, because of their transgressions, that thy people may not faint in the day of trouble. And whatsoever city thy servants shall enter, and the people of that city receive their testimony, let thy peace and thy salvation be upon that city; that they may gather out of that city the righteous, that they may come forth to Zion, or to her stakes, the places of thine appointment, with songs of everlasting joy; and until this be accomplished, let not thy judgments fall upon that city. (D&C 109:38–40)

Gathering to stakes of Zion will provide a place of peace for the Saints of God in contrast to the wars and tribulations of the world. "There will be here and there a stake, etc., for the gathering of the Saints," the Prophet Joseph Smith said. "Some may have cried peace, but the Saints and the world will have little peace from henceforth. Let this not hinder us from going to the stakes, for God has told us to flee not dallying, or we shall be scattered, one here, another there." The Prophet continued, "There [in the stakes of Zion], your children shall be blessed."[90]

Holy places are not limited to Jackson County, Missouri. Rather, each stake of Zion may become a holy place. Like the sheaves gathered on the harvest floor, stakes provide places for the Saints to find spiritual strength and safety. This is particularly true as temples are dedicated to bless those living within the stakes of Zion.

Another sign of the times is the gathering of the faithful (see D&C 133:4). Elder Dallin H. Oaks taught:

> In the early years of this last dispensation, a gathering to Zion involved various locations in the United States: to Kirtland, to Missouri, to Nauvoo, and to the tops of the mountains. Always these were gatherings to prospective temples. With the creation of stakes and the construction of temples in most nations with sizeable populations of the faithful, the current commandment is not to gather to one place but to gather in stakes in our own homelands. There the faithful can enjoy the full blessings of eternity in a house of the Lord. There, in their own homelands, they can obey the Lord's command to enlarge the borders of His people and strengthen her stakes (see D&C 101:21; 133:9, 14). In this way, the stakes of Zion are "for a defense, and for a refuge from the storm, and from wrath when it shall be poured out without mixture upon the whole earth" (D&C 115:6).[91]

It appears that righteous Saints who have gathered to stakes will be protected from the major and minor horrors and wickedness of the last days by the bulwarks of the Zion communities—that is, the Lord revealed places of refuge to escape the terrors of the last days, and we have much to look forward to. Do not misunderstand: the Saints are in for a rough time, but if they, in any given area, will live righteously, they and their families will not suffer the consequences of community wickedness, and, united together, they will be able to meet the challenges of tribulations that will come their way.

Which of the Ten Virgins Will You Be?

Of all of the Savior's teachings concerning preparation for the Second Coming, the parable of the ten virgins seems to be the most poignant. Christ likened latter-day members of His restored Church to ten virgins: "And then, at that day, before the Son of Man comes, the kingdom of heaven shall be likened unto ten virgins" (JST, Matthew 25:1). The admonition to have oil in our lamps is synonymous with being prepared for the Lord's return. Prophets, apostles, and members have shared many interpretations and applications of the valued oil to keep our lamps burning. The Savior Himself referred to those who foresaw the need to have ample oil as being "wise" in contrast with those he called "foolish," who allowed their lamps to burn out without forethought for needed future oil (see Matthew 25:2). "For they that are wise," He explained, are they that "have received the truth, and have taken the Holy Spirit for their guide, and have not been deceived" (D&C 45:57).

Living principles of the gospel can be understood as adding oil to our lamps. President Spencer W. Kimball likened daily righteous living to adding oil to our lamps one drop at a time. He mentioned areas of obtaining oil, such as attendance at sacrament meetings, fasting, family prayer, home teaching, control of bodily appetites, preaching the gospel, studying the scriptures, deeds of kindness, payments of tithes and offerings, chaste thoughts and actions, marriage in the covenant for eternity; "these, too, contribute importantly to the oil with which we can at midnight refuel our exhausted lamps."[92]

Clearly, the Lord expects members of His Church to be valiant in their testimony, living the gospel, and building His kingdom. However, two additional aspects of the parable are worth reflection. First, anciently, lamps were small clay containers filled with oil, and they had a cotton wick that needed to be trimmed (to cut off the burnt end) after each use so it would not smoke when lit again. Even better was to keep the lamp continuously burning day and night, for it was a difficult labor to rekindle a flame, and the burning lamp could provide fire for whatever purpose was needed. Just as the continuously burning lamp is better, there is strength in continuous righteousness.

No good will come in having a lapse in Church activity or in taking a vacation from obeying the commandments. Those who remove themselves from the blessings of the gospel with the intent of returning to Church activity at a later date may find it difficult to symbolically rekindle the flame in their lamp. That is a good message for all to remember in the trials and challenges of life. Further, my experience suggests that most of those who leave Church activity do so for one of two reasons: sin or hurt feelings. If one allows sin or hurt feelings to douse the flame in their lamp or to burn the oil without room in the heart for replenishing, they will be sorrowful when the door to the wedding feast is closed and they are unable to enter.

An important meaning in the parable deals with the stark message of the number of members who will not be prepared for the Savior when He returns. Elder Dallin H. Oaks said:

> Given in the 25th chapter of Matthew, this parable contrasts the circumstances of the five foolish and the five wise virgins. All ten were invited to the wedding feast, but only half of them were prepared with oil in their lamps when the bridegroom came. The five who were prepared went into the marriage feast, and the door was shut. The five who had delayed their preparations came late. The door had been closed, and the Lord denied them entrance, saying, "I know you not" (Matt. 25:12). "Watch therefore," the Savior concluded, "for ye know neither the day nor the hour wherein the Son of man cometh" (Matt. 25:13).
>
> The arithmetic of this parable is chilling. The ten virgins obviously represent members of Christ's Church, for all were invited to the wedding feast and all knew what was required to be admitted when the bridegroom came. But only half were ready when he came.[93]

It seems prudent for each individual to ask, "If I continue on my present course in life, which of the ten virgins will I be? What will the Savior say to me when I approach the door to enter into the wedding feast?"

8
SIGNS OF THE LAST HOURS

ALL SIGNS OF CHRIST'S SECOND Coming are not equal. Even the more casual observer of the signs of the times is often aware that certain events are more indicative that the time is short than are others. Recall the signs of the Savior's birth given to the people in America: "And it came to pass that in the commencement of the ninety and second year [the year of the Savior's birth according the reckoning of the Nephites], behold, the prophecies of the prophets began to be fulfilled more fully; for there began to be greater signs and greater miracles wrought among the people" (3 Nephi 1:4). Similar to the "greater signs" given to the Nephites of the Savior's birth, there are signs of the Second Coming that indicate more than the generality of living in the last days. These signs pertain to the imminent appearances of the Savior and might be termed as *signs of the last hour or hours* rather than signs of the last days.

I expect that as attention-getting as the next earthquake and accompanying tsunami will be, an announcement that two prophets have begun to preach and testify to the people of Jerusalem will ignite greater concern for preparing in earnest for Christ's return. Similarly, suppose that at the next general conference the president of the Church announced the building of the temple in New Jerusalem: Independence, Missouri. I have no doubt that many would sit a little straighter in their seats to hear the counsel for the rest of general conference. If, as has been the case with similar announcements in the past, the New Jerusalem Temple were announced in the Saturday morning session of conference, I can only imagine that the word would spread across the globe before noon to many of those who had not been listening. I predict that following such announcements the topics of the signs of the last days and the Second Coming would receive much more attention in conversations and Church classes in the following months.

The Lord has not revealed in detail a perfect chronology of events or the amount of time between events in the symbolic last hours leading up to His appearances on Mount Zion, the Mount of Olives, and the clouds of heaven. On the other hand, He has indicated which particular signs announce that His coming is imminent. In His Olivet Discourse, the Savior gave signs that indicate the last hour has come. He included the preaching of the gospel to all nations, the abomination of desolation, the sun, moon, and stars darkened, and one last great sign in the heavens. In addition, John the Revelator referred to seven last plagues that would destroy the wicked in conjunction with the Second Coming.

Witness to the World

Seemingly, one of the most telling signs in which the Latter-day Saints are intimately involved is that of taking the message of the Restoration of the gospel to every nation of the world. The Savior told His meridian-day disciples that "the Gospel of the Kingdom shall be preached in all the world, for a witness unto all nations, and then shall the end come, or the destruction of the wicked" (Joseph Smith—Matthew 1:31). The fulfillment of this prophecy will certainly be greater than Moses parting the Red Sea or the walls of Jericho tumbling to the ground.

Today, there are yet many nations and peoples that do not have the opportunity to hear missionaries preach the gospel. Government leaders and prejudices hamper recognition of the Church of Jesus Christ in many nations. Millions upon millions of good people live in these nations, such as Muslim faith–based nations, and do not have the opportunity to accept the gospel. Other honorable people live in nations in turmoil or are under strong antireligious governments. For example, how marvelous will it be to hear an announcement that missionaries are proselyting in Iran or Saudi Arabia?

When Brigham Young University built the prominent Jerusalem Center for Near Eastern Studies on the hillside southeast of the Old City, the Church signed an agreement that those students attending the center would not attempt to proselyte. That agreement eventually extended to any member of the Church living in or visiting the Holy Land. When my family lived in Jerusalem, we were not allowed to answer even simple questions regarding our beliefs posed to us by seemingly sincere people. This prohibition against saying anything about our faith applied not only to Jews but also to the Palestinians—Muslim and Christian. As a result, even those who curiously sought to attend Sabbath worship meetings were turned away. One time while we were among the shop owners in the Old City of Jerusalem, we were asked about our faith as Mormons, and we had to explain that we were not permitted to share anything regarding our beliefs. The shop owner broke into a smile and said, "Let me show you something." He then opened a curtain that revealed a bookshelf full of literature regarding the Church and the Restoration of the gospel. He indicated that government leaders could prevent us from speaking to him, but they could not prevent him from seeking information. Similarly, we had others indicate to us that they had accessed information on the Internet so they could learn more. These experiences and others have opened the door to questions regarding what the Lord meant with the phrase "a witness unto all nations" (Joseph Smith—History 1:31). Could the gospel witness be given via the Internet, radio, television, etc.?

At a fireside in Kirtland, Ohio, Elder Jeffrey R. Holland addressed the need for taking the gospel to all the world before the Lord will return in glory to reign on the earth. Citing the above passage from Joseph Smith—Matthew, he explained that he and others of the Quorum of the Twelve Apostles had discussed their responsibility to spread the message of the Restoration into every nation. In particular, he noted the phrase "for a witness unto all nations" (Joseph Smith—History 1:31). He shared that the Twelve had gone forward and would continue to go forward to give a witness to all nations but that he was not sure what the Lord required for a witness. He explained that the Twelve intended to continue to meet with government leaders of various nations, open doors to missionaries, dedicate lands for the preaching of the gospel, open doors through media and Internet, and set about any other means the Lord might place into their hands.[94] This particular sign of the nearness of the Lord's return bears special importance because the Lord taught His ancient disciples that after the witness is given to the world, "then shall the end come, or the destruction of the wicked" (Joseph Smith—History 1:31).

Seven Last Plagues

"We know that thou has spoken by the mouth of thy prophets terrible things concerning the wicked, in the last days—that thou wilt pour out thy judgments, without measure; therefore, O Lord, deliver thy people from the calamity of the wicked," the Prophet Joseph Smith cried to God in the dedicatory prayer of the Kirtland Temple (D&C 109:45–46). In his apocalyptic vision, the Apostle John wrote, "I saw another sign in heaven, great and marvelous, seven angels having *seven last plagues*; for in them is filled up the wrath of God" (Revelation 15:1; emphasis added). As each of the seven angels poured out vials filled with the wrath of God, the resultant plagues included the following:

1. "Grievous sore[s] upon the men which had the mark of the beast" (Revelation 16:2)
2.&3. Death in the seas, rivers, and fountains of waters (see Revelation 16:3–4)
4. Scorching heat (see Revelation 16:8–9)
5. Pains and sores specifically suffered by the wicked—possibly separating the righteous from the wicked, similar to many of the plagues in the days of Moses and the Egyptians (see Revelation 16:10–11)
6. Kings of all the earth gathering armies together "to the battle of that great day of God Almighty . . . into a place called in the Hebrew tongue Armageddon" (Revelation 16:14, 16)
7. Thunders, lightnings, and "a great earthquake, such as was not since men were upon the earth, so mighty an earthquake, and so great . . . and the cities of the nations fell . . . And every island fled away, and the mountains were not found. And there fell upon men a great hail out of heaven . . . and men blasphemed God because of the plague of the hail; for the plague thereof was exceeding great" (Revelation 16:18–21)

These last plagues appear to be those the Lord referred to as "wrath when it shall be poured out *without mixture* upon the whole earth" (D&C 115:6; emphasis added). The meaning being that these plagues will not be watered down but will come in full force upon the wicked to their destruction. The Lord warned the Saints to assemble during the times of these plagues, "that the gathering together upon the land of Zion, and upon her stakes, may be for a defense, and for a refuge from the storm" (D&C 115:6).

The Lord called upon members of the newly organized Church to "be gathered in unto one place upon the face of this land, to prepare their hearts and be prepared in all things against the day when tribulation and desolation are sent forth upon the wicked" (D&C 29:8). In that same revelation, He included additional details regarding the last plagues. The first plagues John saw poured out upon the earth brought grievous sores, heat, and pain upon the people. There appears to be some connection to the Lord's words that He will "send forth flies upon the face of the earth, which shall take hold of the inhabitants thereof, and shall eat their flesh, and shall cause maggots to come in upon them; and their tongues shall be stayed that they shall not utter against me; and their flesh shall fall from off their bones, and their eyes from their sockets; and it shall come to pass that the beasts of the forest and the fowls of the air shall devour them up" (D&C 29:18–20). Further, this may also refer to the aforementioned "overflowing scourge" in which "a desolating sickness shall cover the land" (D&C 45:31).

Neither John's brief description nor the more explicit latter-day revelation paints a very pleasant picture. The plagues of the last hours are similar to earlier plagues poured out upon the Egyptians—lice, flies, and festering boils (see Exodus 8 and 9). Apparently, the results will also be similar in that the Pharaoh-type individuals of the last hours will yet harden their hearts against God, refusing to turn to Him. On the other hand, modern counterparts to the Israelites will wait upon the Lord to deliver them. Modern-day lands of Goshen will separate the Saints from the biblical Egyptian-like destructions that will primarily come upon the wicked. However, the Lord also warned, "Zion shall escape if she observe to do all things whatsoever I have commanded her. But if she observe not to do whatsoever I have commanded her, I will visit her according to all her works, with sore affliction, with pestilence, with plague, with sword, with vengeance, with devouring fire" (D&C 97:25–26).

The last two plagues need to receive individual discussion as there has been more detail revealed regarding their fulfillment.

Armageddon

The very mention of Armageddon is laden with images of great armies clashing in one last final battle before the Second Coming. Indeed, Armageddon is known and referred to by even the ungodly as the ultimate cataclysm and destruction on earth. Ironically, the word *Armageddon* only appears in scripture one time in one verse of the Bible. John referred to it as the location to which armies of the earth will gather in consequence of spirits of devils influencing wicked leaders and peoples (see Revelation 16:12–16). God's foreknowledge of the extreme wickedness in the last days led Him to triumphantly foreordain the symbolic Armageddon as the time and place in which the wicked come to know His power prior to their utter destruction.

Prophets of the Old Testament—Isaiah, Jeremiah, Ezekiel, Daniel, Joel, Zephaniah, and Zechariah—wrote of the destruction of the wicked in a final, great conflict of armies clashing without regard to the blood and horror of the war in which they engage.[95] In addition, John, in New Testament times, added his witness of the sixth plague poured out upon the earth in the symbolic battle of Armageddon. The detail recorded by these prophets gives reason to accept that the battle of Armageddon is not simply symbolic of wars in the last days but also refers to a specific gathering of armies to battle in Palestine. Their words are passionate, and the reader can feel the intensity of their attempts to paint a picture of the visions they saw. Consider their descriptions as we attempt to capture the scene laid before them.

Isaiah's portrayal poetically displayed the destruction during Armageddon as "the noise of a multitude in the mountains, like a great people; a tumultuous noise of the kingdoms of nations gathered together: the Lord of hosts mustereth the host of the battle. They come from a far country, from the end of heaven, even the Lord, and the weapons of his indignation, to destroy the whole land. Howl ye; for the day of the Lord is at hand; it shall come as a destruction from the Almighty" (Isaiah 13:4–6). "For the indignation of the Lord is upon all nations," Isaiah wrote, "and his fury upon all their armies: he hath utterly destroyed them, he hath delivered them to the slaughter. Their slain also shall be cast out, and their stink shall come up out of their carcases" (Isaiah 34:2–3).

The Lord spoke to the Prophet Joseph Smith of a time of wars. "I have sworn in my wrath," the Lord declared, "and decreed wars upon the face of the earth, and the wicked shall slay the wicked, and fear shall come upon every man" (D&C 63:33). Armageddon appears to be the culmination of all wars that have ever been waged on the earth.

The Lord spoke to Jeremiah of the nations and peoples surrounding the city of Jerusalem and the ancient land of Judah. Following a long and detailed list of Judah's ancient enemies, the Lord declared, "Evil shall go forth from nation to nation. . . . [And] at that day from one end of the earth even unto the other end of the earth: they shall not be lamented, neither gathered, nor buried; but shall be dung upon the ground" (Jeremiah 25:32–33).

The prophets Ezekiel, Daniel, Joel, and Zephaniah detail, often in symbolic terms, those who will play a part in the gathering of armies for this monumental war. Volumes have been written seeking to interpret their words into specific alliances of nations. Most often, little lasting proper interpretation can be gained from those attempts. Rather, their motivation served to liken the prophets' words to themselves and the context of events in their own lifetime. What is evident is that nations will gather against Judah and Jerusalem, where the Lord will make bare His arm before the eyes of all that inhabit the earth. Those in the opposing armies and allied peoples will be destroyed.

The Lord revealed the latter-day enemies of Judah as led by "Gog, the land of Magog, the chief prince of Meshech and Tubal" (Ezekiel 38:2). The allusion to the sons of Japheth, one of Noah's three sons, is readily apparent. They are listed as "Gomer, and *Magog*, and Madai, and Javan, and *Tubal*, and *Meshech,* and Tiras" (Genesis 10:2; emphasis added). Clearly, the message rings that these are not descendants of Noah's firstborn, Shem, forefather of Semitic peoples, including the house of Israel. Rather, they are associated with the people of the land north of Israel and the fertile crescent of the ancient Near East. During the Old Testament times in which Ezekiel lived and prophesied, he and the remnant of Judah were taken captive to Babylon, near these descendants of Japeth. Further, the names of Magog, Meshech, and Tubal referred to peoples in Asia Minor. Meshech is "generally identified with Mushki of Assyrian, and Moschoi of classical sources." Together, Meshech and Tubal "denote the land of central Anatolia and its peoples."[96] In summary, Magog, Meshech, and Tubal were ancient inhabits of northern Asia Minor and the Old Testament fertile crescent, which includes parts of modern-day Turkey, Syria, and Iraq. Ezekiel also aligned Persia and Gomer of the same area with the coalition of nations that will fight against Judah (Ezekiel 38:5–6), alluding to the land of modern-day Iran. In addition, Ezekiel mentioned the peoples of Ethiopia and Libya as coming with the armies of Gog from the lands of northern Asian Minor (Ezekiel 38:5).

Present-day association of these ancient nations with those in which modern cultures have predominantly adopted the Islam religion offers bountiful opportunity to surmise and speculate the causes and alliances of nations that will gather against the Lord's ancient covenant people. Since the creation of the modern state of Israel, nations in Asia Minor and northern Africa have aligned to oppose Israel. Rhetoric rises from their leaders like waves climbing up the beach sands only to fall back again. Again and again, speech-making politicians and would-be leaders attempt to rally multitudes by claiming Israel as their common enemy and declaring their intentions to drive the citizens of Israel into the sea. These claims and growing tensions may lead to the biblical prophecy's fulfillment. On the other hand, the references may be more symbolic of heathen or non-Jewish nations of the world than of specific geography.

Speaking to Gog, the Lord declared, "Thou shalt come from thy place out of the north parts, thou, and many people with thee . . . a great company, and a mighty army: and thou shalt come up against my people of Israel, as a cloud to cover the land; it shall be in the latter days, and I will bring thee against my land, that the heathen may know me, when I shall be sanctified in thee, O Gog, before their eyes" (Ezekiel 38:15–16). Gog will fail in his attempts to take the land of Israel when the Lord will "go forth, and fight against those nations . . . [and] will smite all the people that have fought against Jerusalem" (Zechariah 14:3, 12).

Nephi saw the same latter-day events revealed to John the Revelator regarding the prophecies of Armageddon (see 1 Nephi 14:18–25). Nephi associated the destruction Ezekiel prophesied with the great and abominable church—the mother of harlots—shown to John as "the great whore that sitteth upon many waters: with whom the kings of the earth have committed fornication" (Revelation 17:1–2). Further, Nephi saw in vision that "the blood of that great and abominable church, which is the whore of all the earth, shall turn upon their own heads; for they shall war among themselves. . . . And all that fight against Zion shall be destroyed, and that great whore, who hath perverted the right ways of the Lord, yea, that great and abominable church, shall tumble to the dust and great shall be the fall of it" (1 Nephi 22:13–14). "For the day soon cometh," Nephi continued, "that all the proud and they that do wickedly shall be as stubble; and the day cometh that they must be burned" (1 Nephi 22:15).

It is evident that God's contention against Gog and the land of Magog is not their ethnicity, nationality, ancestry, or geographic location but rather that they are proud and wicked. Similarly, Zion does not denote a nation, Jewish or otherwise, but instead denotes those who are pure in heart (see D&C 97:21). One thing is sure: "the fullness of the wrath of God shall be poured out upon all the children of men; for he will not suffer that the wicked shall destroy the righteous" (1 Nephi 22:16). Indeed, Nephi is emphatic on this point. He repeatedly assured his readers that "the righteous need not fear" (1 Nephi 22:17, 22), for "they shall be saved, even if it so be as by fire" (1 Nephi 22:17).

The prophetic storyline of the physical battle of Armageddon will continue to develop into a new chapter, detailing the fulfillment of the "abomination of desolation" (Joseph Smith—Matthew 1:32) and will conclude with the Savior's appearance on the Mount of Olives to the Jewish remnant. Those particulars will be discussed later in chapter 11.

A Great Earthquake and Hailstorm

The last plague seen in vision by the Apostle John that will be poured out on the wicked world to its destruction will be a dual punch of a great earthquake and a horrific hailstorm (Revelation 16:18–20). It seems appropriate to interpret John's record as meaning there is to be a single earthquake and, likewise, one hailstorm that fulfills this visionary event. However, there will be earthquakes and hailstorms that precede them as more general signs of the times; these two specific signs are the earthquake and hailstorm of the last hours before the Savior comes to reign on the earth.

In latter-day revelation, the Lord referred to the hailstorm as "a great hailstorm sent forth to destroy the crops of the earth" (D&C 29:16). The grand earthquake is described as "such as was not since men were upon the earth, so mighty an earthquake, and so great" (Revelation 16:18). John associated the fall of cities with this earthquake, specifically the great city of Jerusalem being "divided into three parts" (Revelation 16:19). In his vision, John also saw that "every island fled away, and the mountains were not found" (Revelation 16:20). It was possibly due to these great changes that the Prophet Joseph Smith wrote the inspired description of the Lord's voice being manifested as a voice "which shall break down the mountains, and the valleys shall not be found" (D&C 133:22). "He shall command the great deep," the Prophet continued, "and it shall be driven back into the north countries, and the islands shall become one land" (D&C 133:23).

The events associated with the great earthquake are so remarkable that they challenge our minds. Not since the creation of the earth have such dramatic changes occurred in gathering the waters and the dry land (see Moses 2:9–10). Then again, the Lord referred to the changes preceding the Millennium as creating "new heavens and a new earth" (Isaiah 65:17).[97]

Addressing those who find these prophecies too incredible to believe, Peter wrote

> that in the last days there shall come scoffers, walking after their own lusts. Denying the Lord Jesus Christ, and saying, Where is the promise of his coming? For since the fathers fell asleep, all things must continue as they are, and have continued as they are from the beginning of the creation. For this they willingly are ignorant of, that of old the heavens, and the earth standing in water and out of the water, were created by the word of God. . . . But the day of the Lord will come as a thief in the night, in the which the heavens shall shake, and the earth also shall tremble, and the mountains shall melt, and pass away with a great noise (JST, 2 Peter 3:3–5, 10).

Signs in the Heavens and the Sign of the Coming of the Son of Man

There will have been previous signs in the heavens, but those of the last hour will occur after the general tribulations and immediately before the Savior appears in glory. In one of the rare references to a chronological order of events leading to His Second Coming, the Savior referred to that which will immediately follow the tribulations of the last days. "The sun shall be darkened," He declared, "and the moon shall not give her light, and the stars shall fall from heaven, and the powers of heaven shall be shaken" (Joseph Smith—Matthew 1:33).

Indicating what we might anticipate in the fulfillment of these prophetic words, on November 13, 1833, the Prophet Joseph Smith wrote:

> About 4 o'clock a.m. I was awakened by Brother Davis knocking at my door, and calling on me to arise and behold the signs in the heavens. I arose, and to my great joy, beheld the stars fall from heaven like a shower of hailstones; a literal fulfillment of the word of God, as recorded in the holy Scriptures, and a sure sign that the coming of Christ is close at hand. In the midst of this shower of fire, I was led to exclaim, "How marvelous are Thy works, O Lord! I thank Thee for Thy mercy unto Thy servant; save me in Thy kingdom for Christ's sake. Amen."

The appearance of these signs varied in different sections of the country: In Zion, all heaven seemed enwrapped in splendid fireworks, as if every star in the broad expanse had been suddenly hurled from its course, and sent lawless through the wilds of ether. Some at times appeared like bright shooting meteors, with long trains of light following in their course, and in numbers resembled large drops of rain in sunshine. These seemed to vanish when they fell behind the trees, or came near the ground. Some of the long trains of light following the meteoric stars, were visible for some seconds; these streaks would curl and twist up like serpents writhing. The appearance was beautiful, grand, and sublime beyond description; and it seemed as if the artillery and fireworks of eternity were set in motion to enchant and entertain the Saints, and terrify and awe the sinners of the earth. Beautiful and terrific as was the scenery, it will not fully compare with the time when the sun shall become black like sack-cloth of hair, the moon like blood, and the stars fall to the earth—Rev. vi:13.[98]

Perhaps the last sign given to earth's inhabitants preceding the Savior's appearance to the world will be "a great sign in heaven, and all people shall see it together" (D&C 88:93). In the Olivet Discourse, the Savior referred to it as "the sign of the Son of Man in heaven" (Joseph Smith—Matthew 1:36). At the April 1843 conference of the Church, the Prophet Joseph Smith testified: "There will be wars and rumors of wars, signs in the heavens above and on the earth beneath, the sun turned into darkness and the moon to blood, earthquakes in divers places, the seas heaving beyond their bounds; then will appear one grand sign of the Son of Man in heaven. But what will the world do? They will say it is a planet, a comet, etc. But the Son of Man will come as the sign of the coming of the Son of Man, which will be as the light of the morning cometh out of the east."[99]

9
WHERE WILL THE SAVIOR APPEAR AND TO WHOM?

WHEN YOU THINK OF THE SECOND Coming of Christ, what do you see? Often one envisions a single event in which the Savior comes in great glory in the clouds of heaven, accompanied by angels, to divide the righteous from the wicked. Although such a view is somewhat accurate, it is not complete. One of the aspects regarding the Second Coming clarified in the revelations of the Restoration is that the Second Coming consists of several separate appearances. That is, the Savior has revealed that in ushering in the Millennium, He will appear in several different locations and to distinct and specific groups of people. Thus, to better understand the Second Coming we must consider the various different appearances and events that comprise the Lord's Second Coming.

In a rather general outline of Christ's appearances, the Prophet Joseph Smith referred in revelation to a time "when the Lamb shall stand upon Mount Zion and with him a hundred and forty-four thousand, having the Father's name written on their foreheads. Wherefore, prepare for the coming of the Bridegroom; go ye, go ye out to meet him. For behold, he shall stand upon the mount of Olivet, and upon the mighty ocean, even the great deep, and upon the islands of the sea, and upon the land of Zion" (D&C 133:18–20). Elder Bruce R. McConkie explained that these references make the meaning of the Savior's Second Coming clear "that there will be many appearances, in many places, to many people."[100] To quickly summarize, no one single appearance of the Savior constitutes the Second Coming. Rather, it is more appropriate to refer to the several appearances of the Savior together as comprising the Second Coming.

President Ezra Taft Benson divided the Savior's appearances into visits to three groups of peoples:

His first appearances will be to the righteous Saints who have gathered to the New Jerusalem. In this place of refuge they will be safe from the wrath of the Lord, which will be poured out without measure on all nations. . . .

The second appearance of the Lord will be to the Jews. To these beleaguered sons of Judah, surrounded by hostile Gentile armies, who again threaten to overrun Jerusalem, the Savior—their Messiah—will appear and set His feet on the Mount of Olives, "and it shall cleave in twain, and the earth shall tremble, and reel to and fro, and the heavens also shall shake" (D&C 45:48).

The Lord himself will then rout the Gentile armies, decimating their forces (see Ezek. 38, 39). Judah will be spared, no longer to be persecuted and scattered. . . .

The third appearance of Christ will be to the rest of the world. . . .

All nations will see Him "in the clouds of heaven, clothed with power and great glory; with all the holy angels; . . .

"And the Lord shall utter his voice, and all the ends of the earth shall hear it; and the nations of the earth shall mourn, and they that have laughed shall see their folly.

"And calamity shall cover the mocker, and the scorner shall be consumed; and they that have watched for iniquity shall be hewn down and cast into the fire" (D&C 45:44, 49–50).

Yea, come He will![101]

Significantly, rather than referring to a single appearance, President Benson referred to the Savior's appearances to the Saints alone in plural. For example, in addition to appearing to the Saints in the New Jerusalem, there is another event that ought to also be included. Elder Bruce R. McConkie explained:

Before the Lord Jesus descends openly and publicly in the clouds of glory, attended by all the hosts of heaven; before the great and dreadful day of the Lord sends terror and destruction from one end of the earth to the other; before he stands on Mount Zion, or sets his feet on Olivet, or utters his voice from an American Zion or a Jewish

Jerusalem; before all flesh shall see him together; before any of his appearances, which taken together comprise the second coming of the Son of God—before all these, there is to be a secret appearance to selected members of his Church. He will come in private to his prophet and to the apostles then living. Those who have held keys and powers and authorities in all ages from Adam to the present will also be present. . . . And it will take place in Daviess County, Missouri, at a place called Adam-ondi-Ahman.[102]

Before examining these various foretold visits, it is important to note that, in general, taken together, the appearances of the Second Coming of Christ have a major purpose of ushering in the millennial conditions that will prevail for a thousand years. However, in addition, each individual appearance will have important unique and specific purposes toward accomplishing the general objective of preparing for millennial glory. Obviously, we do not claim to comprehend all things regarding the purposes of the Savior's appearances. However, we can explore the revelations and gain a clearer understanding of the Lord's plans and our place as His servants in preparing for those great events.

As we study the scriptures or teachings of latter-day prophets, it is imperative that we keep clear in our mind which appearance is referred to. For example, as explained, the Savior will appear at Adam-ondi-Ahman before He appears to the Jewish remnant on the Mount of Olives or in glory in the clouds of heaven to the world. How much time will elapse between the appearances is not specified in the scriptures. Thus, which signal events of the last days will occur between the Savior's appearances is also often unspecified.

Consider, for instance, the following areas of indeterminable chronology of events. The prophesied future temple in Jerusalem may be built after the Savior's private appearance to the Jewish remnant on the Mount of Olives but before His appearance to the world. Further, the building of the temple in Jackson County, Missouri, most definitely will take place before the appearance of the Savior at that location but possibly after the gathering of Saints from all dispensations at Adam-ondi-Ahman. Another example is the sequence of events from the lost ten tribes returning to the appearances of the Savior. It is unknown whether the ten tribes will return before the Savior appears at Adam-ondi-Ahman or whether it will be sometime after. Along that same line, will the ten tribes return before the Savior appears to the world but after He appears to the Jewish remnant? So many events are closely tied together, but it is hard to say which will come first or which will be important to fulfill before another one can come to pass.

Additionally, if we do not separate the various appearances of the Savior, we may miss that some events could happen decades apart. There are some indicators in the revelations regarding time associations of one event to another that provide insight for the careful student of the scriptures. Even so, caution is advised in making definite declarations beyond the clearly spelled out signs, lest we be caught in the same condition as the Jews of the meridian day, who missed the significance of the monumental events fulfilling prophecy in their day. Understanding all of the prophesied events and conditions provides a picture that can be put together one puzzle piece at a time, especially as the events transpire. Consequently, a study of the prophecies surrounding each of the Savior's appearances will definitely prove to be of great value.

10
APPEARANCES TO THE SAINTS

Preparing for the Savior's Coming to Adam-ondi-Ahman

THE SAVIOR'S RETURN TO THE earth carries great importance for individuals on both sides of the veil because there are more Saints in the spirit world anticipating the coming of the Lord to usher in the millennial day than there are here in mortality. There are also untold numbers of the faithful who have been resurrected and who await the time when they will return with the Savior in glory. It is proper, then, that the Savior's first major appearance on the earth will include mortals, postmortal spirits, and resurrected beings.

The appointed place for this gathering of Saints from both sides of the veil has been identified as Adam-ondi-Ahman, located in present-day northwestern Missouri. The Prophet Joseph Smith designated the location of Adam-ondi-Ahman while visiting an area known as Spring Hill in Daviess County, Missouri, on May 19, 1838. "Spring Hill is named by the Lord Adam-ondi-Ahman," Joseph said, "because, said he, it is the place where Adam shall come to visit his people, or the Ancient of Days shall sit, as spoken of by Daniel the prophet" (D&C 116). Early Saints settled this area of northwestern Missouri in 1838 and surveyed it for a city-stake of Zion. Along with other Saints, those in Spring Hill were soon after driven from Missouri as a result of Missouri Governor Lilburn W. Boggs's extermination order. Since that time, the Church has purchased much of the original settlement of these early Saints and the nearby valley bordered by the Grand River, recognizing them as essential sites regarding future important events.

The scriptures are clear that before the Savior comes to those assembled at Adam-ondi-Ahman, precise preparation will be necessary. The Prophet Joseph Smith taught that Adam, the first man on earth, will return to prepare his posterity to receive the Savior in glory and to set up a kingdom ready to receive the Lord. Joseph said that Adam

> will call his children together and hold a council with them to prepare them for the coming of the Son of Man. He (Adam) is the father of the human family, and presides over the spirits of all men, and all that have had the keys must stand before him in this grand council. . . . The Son of Man stands before him, and there is given him glory and dominion. Adam delivers up his stewardship to Christ, that which was delivered to him as holding the keys of the universe, but retains his standing as head of the human family.[103]

The answers to many questions regarding the Savior's return to Adam-ondi-Ahman remain to be revealed. Consequently, at times, in discussions regarding the Second Coming, the door is unwisely opened to wild speculation concerning the prophesied events to occur there. Clearly, the safest course to pursue in discussing Adam-ondi-Ahman is to examine the prophecy of Daniel using prophetic commentary and to allow speculative ideas to fall to the wayside while awaiting further revelation and clarification from the president of the Lord's Church.

The Bible preserves that Daniel recorded a vision wherein the degenerate kingdoms of the earth were represented by four beasts. Each of these earthly kingdoms or empires had their season of dominion, which was taken away by the succeeding kingdom. Finally, Daniel saw that in the last days, the Lord God would set up a kingdom that was never to be destroyed. Describing his vision of these events, Daniel said, "I beheld till the thrones [of the earthly governments] were cast down, and the Ancient of days [Adam] did sit, whose garment was white as snow, and the hair of his head like the pure wool: his throne was like the fiery flame, and his wheels as burning fire" (Daniel 7:9). This description of Adam in his prophesied return is similar to that given of the Savior during His appearance to Joseph Smith and Oliver Cowdery in the Kirtland Temple. They described the Lord, saying, "His eyes were as a flame of fire; the hair of his head was white like the pure snow; his countenance shone above the brightness of the sun" (D&C 110:3). Thus, it appears that Daniel saw the then future Father Adam as a glorified resurrected being. Adam will govern the latter-day kingdom of God as its prince, reigning under the direction of the King Jesus Christ.

Adam's Responsibility in Preparing for the Second Coming of Jesus Christ

It may be well to pause for a moment in the description of the events to occur at Adam-ondi-Ahman to review the responsibilities the Lord gave Adam relating to the latter days. Elder Bruce R. McConkie observed, "If we are to understand what shall transpire at Adam-ondi-Ahman in the near future, we must first envision the relationship between the Lord Jehovah, who is Christ our Savior, and the man Adam."[104]

Jesus Christ is the Firstborn Spirit Son of God and the Only Begotten Son of God in the flesh. He created worlds without number under the Father's direction. Further, the Father committed into the hands of Jehovah the responsibility for bringing to pass the immortality and eternal life of all of the Father's children throughout His creations. Christ presides over innumerable earths under the direction of His Father. On the other hand, the Lord revealed that Michael's, or Adam's, place in the heavenly order of the priesthood is to preside over all of his and Eve's posterity upon this earth and that Adam presides under the direction of Christ, "who hath appointed Michael your prince, and established his feet, and set him upon high, and given unto him the keys of salvation under the counsel and direction of the Holy One, who is without beginning of days or end of life" (D&C 78:16).

Adam has the responsibility to supervise and direct God's work regarding the salvation of His children on earth through all generations. In the scriptures, Adam is referred to not only as an angel of God but as the archangel, meaning that Adam, or Michael, is the chief or head of all other angels. The name *Michael* means "one who is like God." In this instance, the meaning is that Adam has the authority to act in the name of God as God's representative. He is the head of many angels who are servants of God. In premortality, Adam played a prominent role as the archangel. The Apostle John saw that "there was war in heaven: Michael and his angels fought against the dragon [Lucifer]; and the dragon fought and his angels, and prevailed not; neither was their place found any more in heaven. And the great dragon was cast out . . . and his angels were cast out with him" (Revelation 12:7–9). Adam also had important responsibilities in the creation of the earth. "The Priesthood was first given to Adam," the Prophet Joseph Smith explained. "He obtained the First Presidency, and held the keys of it from generation to generation. He obtained it in the Creation, before the world was formed, as in Genesis 1:26, 27, 28. He had dominion given him over every living creature. He is Michael the Archangel, spoken of in the Scriptures."[105]

Adam retained his place of presidency in the priesthood during his mortal life and—important to understanding the events at Adam-ondi-Ahman—after his death. Over the centuries and millennia since the Creation, the Lord Jesus Christ has directed His work on earth through Adam. Joseph Smith said, "The Priesthood is an everlasting principle and existed with God from eternity, and will to eternity, without beginning of days or end of years. The keys [of the priesthood] have to be brought from heaven whenever the Gospel is sent. When they are revealed from heaven, it is by Adam's authority."[106]

Thus, Adam presides over the entire human family of this earth and has been given the keys, or the responsibility, to oversee the administering of the gospel. However, in the eternal order of the priesthood, Adam is a prince who receives direction from the Savior, who, under the direction of the Father, is the King who created and presides over worlds without number.

Regarding Adam's position in the priesthood and his relationship to the priesthood order in the various dispensations of the gospel on earth, the Prophet Joseph Smith stated:

> Commencing with Adam, who was the first man, who is spoken of in Daniel as being the "Ancient of Days," or in other words, the first and oldest of all, the great, grand progenitor of whom it is said in another place he is Michael, because he was the first and father of all, not only by progeny, but the first to hold the spiritual blessings, to whom was made known the plan of ordinances for the salvation of his posterity unto the end, and to whom Christ was first revealed, and through whom Christ has been revealed from heaven, and will continue to be revealed from henceforth. Adam holds the keys of the dispensation of the fullness of times; i.e., the dispensation of all the times have been and will be revealed through him from the beginning to Christ, and from Christ to the end of all the dispensations that are to be revealed.[107]

To hold keys of the priesthood is to be given the power of directing the labors of other priesthood bearers. As previously noted, Adam was given responsibility to direct the work of the priesthood on earth during his lifetime. Further, after Adam died, his responsibilities continued for the plan of salvation on the earth, and he directed the work even from the postmortal spirit world. Thus, he coordinated the work of the priesthood in two spheres: the spirit world and mortality. In addition, over time, various priesthood bearers were translated, such as those of the city of Enoch, Melchizedek's people, and specifically Moses and Elijah. These translations added a third sphere of beings over which Adam presided, which state of affairs continued until the Resurrection of Christ from the grave. We know that many Saints rose from the dead at the time of Christ's Resurrection (see Matthew 27:51–53; 3 Nephi 23:8–12). Thus, after that time, Adam had a fourth sphere, that of resurrected beings from this earth, added to his responsibilities.[108]

At various times, gospel principles and ordinances were lost or changed, depending on the faithfulness or wickedness of the covenant people. Maintaining the consistency of true gospel principles and ordinances is Adam's responsibility. Under his direction, other priesthood bearers have carried out the work of restoration in various dispensations. The gospel of Jesus Christ is eternal. The Prophet Joseph Smith said:

> Therefore He [Christ] set the ordinances to be the same forever and ever, and set Adam to watch over them, to reveal them from heaven to man, or to send angels to reveal them. . . . These angels are under the direction of Michael or Adam, who acts under the direction of the Lord. . . .
>
> This, then, is the nature of the Priesthood; every man holding the Presidency of his dispensation, and one man holding the Presidency of them all, even Adam; and Adam receiving his Presidency and authority from the Lord, but cannot receive a fullness until Christ shall present the Kingdom to the Father, which shall be at the end of the last dispensation.[109]

Adam, who is under the direction of Christ, presides over the Prophet Joseph Smith and others who hold the keys of the kingdom in the last days. Adam will return to the earth and hold a council with those who have held keys, and he will establish an organization to oversee all of God's children in the millennial day. When the Savior returns, such an organization will need to include people on the earth, as well as those who have died and dwell as spirits or have been resurrected. Perfect order will prevail among the various priesthood bearers from all ages. Adam will preside over the uniting of the kingdom of God on earth for the living and the kingdom of God in heaven for those who have passed through the veil.

At that unifying event, many beings will be upon the earth simultaneously for the first time. The Millennium will usher in a time when not only Adam but "Enoch also, and they who were with him; the prophets who were before him; and Noah also, and they who were before him; and Moses also, and they who were before him; and from Moses to Elijah, and from Elijah to John, who were with Christ in his resurrection, and the holy apostles, with Abraham, Isaac, and Jacob, shall be in the presence of the Lamb" (D&C 133:54–55). The initial meetings of these prophets and the Saints of their respective days will be held at Adam-ondi-Ahman in preparation for the millennial reign of Jesus Christ.

In addition, apparently, this gathering preliminary to the appearance of the Savior will include a time of judgment regarding the state of affairs in preparation for Christ's return. "A fiery stream issued and came forth from before him [Adam]," Daniel said. "Thousand thousands ministered unto him, and ten thousand times ten thousand stood before him [Adam]: the judgment was set, and the books were opened" (Daniel 7:2). The kingdom of God will include the worthy of all dispensations, organized in proper priesthood government and extending both geographically across the face of the earth and generationally from Adam through each dispensation and prophetic ministry. Saints from every age will be members of the same Church of Jesus Christ and will be organized with appropriately appointed presiding priesthood officers in their proper places from each dispensation.

In time, all ordinances of the gospel will be performed for every one of Adam's worthy posterity. Adam will deliver his stewardship report to Christ, who will "have subdued all enemies under his feet, and shall have perfected his work; when he shall deliver up the kingdom, and present it unto the Father, spotless" (D&C 76:106–107). Thus, the events at Adam-ondi-Ahman further the work of Christ and will find ultimate fulfillment in a day following the Millennium when we may return to the fullness of the presence of the Father.

Worthy of additional consideration is some indication that the keys of salvation that Michael holds include the authorization to direct the resurrection of the dead. The Lord revealed to Daniel, "And at that time shall Michael stand up, the great prince which standeth for the children of thy people: and there shall be a time of trouble, such as never was since there was a nation even to that same time" (Daniel 12:1). Apparently, this is referring to the time of the battles of Armageddon and the latter-day abomination of desolation in Jerusalem, which will be discussed hereafter in conjunction with the Savior's appearance to the Jews on the Mount of Olives. "And at that time," the Lord continues, "thy people shall be delivered, every one that shall be found written in the book. And many of them that sleep in the dust of the earth shall awake, some to everlasting life, and some to shame and everlasting contempt" (Daniel 12:1–2). Clearly, Michael's involvement in the people's deliverance is not specified in Daniel; however, in latter-day revelation, the Lord clarified Michael's role in calling forth the dead from their graves. "Behold, verily I say unto you, before the earth shall pass away, Michael, mine archangel, shall sound his trump, and then shall all the dead awake, for their graves shall be opened, and they shall come forth—yea, even all" (D&C 29:26).

The sounding of Michael's trump is a symbolic announcement of the resurrection of the dead. The Son of God loosed the bands of death for all through His atoning sacrifice and rising from the tomb. Similar to all of his duties, Adam presides over the salvation of men, including the resurrection, under the Savior's direction. The Prophet Brigham Young taught that the keys for the work of resurrection have not yet been restored to the earth in this dispensation: "We have not, neither can we receive here, the ordinance and the keys of the resurrection. They will be given to those who have passed off this stage of action and have received their bodies again, as many have already done and many more will. They will be ordained, by those who hold the keys of the resurrection, to go forth and resurrect the Saints, just as we receive the ordinance of baptism, then the keys of authority to baptize others for the remission of their sins."[110]

It is altogether appropriate that Adam, who, along with Eve, brought death into the world, would be given the blessing to preside over the raising of his posterity from the grave. The importance of the preparatory meetings and organization at Adam-ondi-Ahman may well include the initiation of the important work of raising the righteous from their graves. On the other hand, it may be that priesthood instruction and organization regarding the resurrection will be all that occurs at that time, rather than the actual calling forth of the dead from their graves. Regardless of the possible scenarios we may contemplate, at present, we must await further prophetic clarification to know with surety the place of Adam and the timing or association of the resurrection with the foretold meetings at Adam-ondi-Ahman.

The Savior Comes to Adam-ondi-Ahman

Evidently, after all the necessary preparations have been attended to at Adam-ondi-Ahman, Christ will come to the Saints who are gathered there. Daniel further wrote, "I saw in the night visions, and, behold, one like the Son of man came with the clouds of heaven, and came to the Ancient of days, and they brought him [Adam] near before him [Christ]. And there was given him [Christ] dominion, and glory, and a kingdom, that all people, nations, and languages, should serve him: his dominion is an everlasting dominion, which shall not pass away, and his kingdom that which shall not be destroyed" (Daniel 7:13–14). One purpose in gathering to Adam-ondi-Ahman is to set up the organization of the Savior's kingdom during the Millennium. We will see a transfer of power from the worldly kingdoms of the fallen earth to the kingdom of God, which will recognize Christ as our King and Lawgiver. Under the Savior's direction, His servants, with Adam at the head, will govern the earth. It does not appear that this will require a confrontation between forces of the world and the Saints. The Lord revealed that previous to this time or shortly thereafter, wars, famines, plagues, earthquakes, and violent storms will chasten the inhabitants of the earth, "until the consumption decreed hath made a full end of all nations" (D&C 87:6).

Daniel added, "I beheld, and the same horn [the last earthly kingdom to have dominion] made war with the saints, and prevailed against them; until the Ancient of days came, and judgment was given to the saints of the most High; and the time came that the saints possessed the kingdom" (Daniel 7:21–22). The Lord commanded His Saints to "be subject to the powers that be, until he reigns whose right it is to reign, and subdues all enemies under his feet" (D&C 58:22). The idea of judgment mentioned in the passage in Daniel refers to government and the power of judging among the nations. The Savior spoke of this time as that which would prevail in the Millennium, "for in mine own due time will I come upon the earth in judgment, and my people shall be redeemed and shall reign with me on earth. For the great Millennium, of which I have spoken by the mouth of my servants, shall come" (D&C 43:29–30).

Daniel identified the initiation of the millennial government with the return of Adam, which most likely refers to the Savior's return to Adam-ondi-Ahman. Thus, we close this chapter of the Savior's appearances, recognizing that relatively precious little has been revealed. Yet, we esteem of great worth the single pearl of Daniel's writings, that in the last days, the Son of Man will come to the Ancient of Days and be given everlasting dominion over the people of the earth, set in the gold band of the revelations to the Prophet Joseph Smith, that Christ will meet with Adam and his righteous posterity at Adam-ondi-Ahman. Surely we must await further revelations and directions, as they will be given to the authorized servants of God to know more concerning the events of Adam-ondi-Ahman. It would be wise to keep our eyes on developments in that land and further explanation of our duties to prepare for these great events.

The Savior on Mount Zion

"The Lamb shall stand upon Mount Zion, and with him a hundred and forty-four thousand, having the Father's name written on their foreheads" (D&C 133:18). Such reveals the sacred word. Where is the location of Mount Zion, and who are the 144,000 who will return here with the Savior? What are the purposes of this appearance and the ministry of the 144,000? The Lord revealed that Mount Zion "shall be the city of New Jerusalem. Which city shall be built, beginning at the temple lot, which is appointed by the finger of the Lord, in the western boundaries of the State of Missouri, and dedicated by the hand of Joseph Smith, Jun., and others with whom the Lord was well pleased" (D&C 84:2–3).

The Book of Mormon prophet Ether saw in vision "that a New Jerusalem should be built up upon this land [the Americas], unto the remnant of the seed of Joseph. . . . Wherefore, the remnant of Joseph shall be built upon this land; and it shall be a land of their inheritance; and they shall build up a holy city unto the Lord, like unto the Jerusalem of old" (Ether 13:6, 8). In the summer of 1831, the Prophet Joseph Smith and other companions traveled to Missouri at the command of the Lord. After their arrival in Jackson County, the Prophet asked the Lord in prayer, "When will Zion be built up in her glory, and where will thy Temple stand, unto which all nations shall come in the last days?"[111] In response to the Prophet's plea, the Lord revealed:

> Hearken, O ye elders of my church, saith the Lord your God, who have assembled yourselves together, according to my commandments, in this land, which is the land of Missouri, which is the land which I have appointed and consecrated for the gathering of my saints. Wherefore, this is the land of promise, and the place for the city of Zion. And thus saith the Lord your God, if you will receive wisdom here is wisdom. Behold, the place which is now called Independence is the

center place; and a spot for the temple is lying westward, upon a lot which is not far from the courthouse. (D&C 57:1–3)

Among all houses of the Lord, the temple to be built at the center place of Zion will stand supreme. The Lord revealed that the gathering to and building of the city of New Jerusalem will have its beginning at "the place of the temple" (D&C 84:4). Along with the companion temple to be built in the Jerusalem of old, this is the temple in which Isaiah's words will find ultimate fulfillment:

> And it shall come to pass in the last days that the mountain of the Lord's house shall be established in the tops of the mountains, and shall be exalted above the hills; and all nations shall flow unto it. And many people shall go and say, Come ye, and let us go up to the mountain of the Lord, to the house of the God of Jacob; and he will teach us of his ways, and we will walk in his paths: for out of Zion shall go forth the law, and the word of the Lord from Jerusalem. (Isaiah 2:2–3)

The 1831 vision for the center of Zion consisted of a complex of twenty-four buildings, all dedicated as houses of the Lord. The buildings were located on a plot map of which Joseph Smith wrote:

> The names of the temples to be built on the painted squares as represented on the plot of the city of Zion, which is now about to be forwarded thither:—numbers 10, 11, and 12, are to be called, House of the Lord, for the Presidency of the High and most Holy Priesthood, after the order of Melchizedek, which was after the order of the Son of God, upon Mount Zion, City of the New Jerusalem. Numbers 7, 8, and 9, the Sacred Apostolic Repository, for the use of the Bishop. Numbers 4, 5, and 6, the Holy Evangelical House, for the High Priesthood of the Holy Order of God. Numbers 1, 2, and 3, the House of the Lord, for the Elders of Zion, an Ensign to the Nations. Numbers 22, 23, and 24, House of the Lord for the Presidency of the High Priesthood, after the Order of Aaron, a Standard for the People. Numbers 19, 20, and 21, House of the Lord, the Law of the Kingdom of Heaven, and Messenger to

the People; for the Highest Priesthood after the Order of Aaron. Numbers 16, 17, and 18, House of the Lord for the Teachers in Zion, Messenger to the Church. Numbers 13, 14, and 15, House of the Lord for the Deacons in Zion, Helps in Government. Underneath must be written on each house—HOLINESS TO THE LORD.[112]

The Prophet Joseph Smith instructed the Saints to commence by building temple number five as the beginning of the city of Zion, which temple was very similar to that built in Kirtland, Ohio (see *HC* 1:359–362). On the other hand, the temple built in Nauvoo had several modifications included to fulfill the additional instructions regarding the administering of sacred ordinances for the living and the dead. After the Saints settled in the Salt Lake Valley, Brigham Young built the center of the city based upon Joseph's instructions and plat for Zion. Since then, continual prophetic direction for Church headquarters in Salt Lake has often supplemented the original design from 1831. Among the additional buildings are the Tabernacle, Assembly Hall, and Church Administration Building, which houses offices for the First Presidency, the Quorum of the Twelve Apostles, and others. In addition, to the east of the Salt Lake Temple, the high-rise Church Office Building houses the offices of the Presiding Bishopric and other Church officers, as well as many employees. Further, surrounding Temple Square, the large Conference Center, Church History Library, Family History Center, Museum of Church History and Art, Relief Society Building, and Joseph Smith Memorial Building have been built.[113] It is possible that the original design for the twenty-four Houses of the Lord may be superseded by others more reflective of the course the Church has taken in Salt Lake City on Temple Square and the blocks surrounding it.

During the Prophet's 1831 visit, the land of Zion was dedicated, as was the site for the latter-day temple in Zion. Because the early Saints did not live worthy of the Lord's blessing, they were unable to build the temple in Jackson County as they had been commanded. Thus, rather than building up Zion according to the ancient promises, they were driven from it. Consequently, today, the question the Prophet Joseph Smith posed to the Lord in 1831 is oft repeated: "When will Zion be built up in her glory?"[114] In an explanatory response President Spencer W. Kimball clarified:

> The length of time required "to accomplish all things pertaining to Zion" is strictly up to us and how we live, for creating Zion

"commences in the heart of each person." (*Journal of Discourses*, 9:283.) That it would take some time to learn our lessons was seen by the prophets. In 1863 Brigham Young stated:

"If the people neglect their duty, turn away from the holy commandments which God has given us, seek their own individual wealth, and neglect the interests of the kingdom of God, we may expect to be here [in the Salt Lake Valley] quite a time—perhaps a period that will be far longer than we anticipate." (*Journal of Discourses*, 11:102.)

Unfortunately we live in a world that largely rejects the values of Zion. Babylon has not and never will comprehend Zion. . . . This state of affairs stands in marked contrast to the Zion the Lord seeks to establish through his covenant people. Zion can be built up only among those who are the pure in heart, not a people torn by covetousness or greed, but a pure and selfless people. Not a people who are pure in appearance, rather a people who are pure in heart. Zion is to be in the world and not of the world, not dulled by a sense of carnal security, nor paralyzed by materialism. No, Zion is not things of the lower, but of the higher order.[115]

Therefore, the Lord waits upon us to become pure in heart, and we await the word of the Lord directing the Saints through the president of the Church to begin the construction of the temple in Zion to which the Savior will return. During the intervening time, we continue to learn to live more Zion-like lives in personal preparation for the Lord's call. At some future day, the Saints will receive the long-anticipated signal to arise and send building materials and workmen to construct the New Jerusalem and the temple of Zion. Whether the other twenty-three buildings will be built before or after the Savior returns, or at all, remains to be revealed.

Will the Saints All Gather to Jackson County, Missouri?

The Savior's appearance on Mount Zion will fulfill Malachi's prophecy: "Behold, I will send my messenger, and he shall prepare the way before me: and the Lord, whom ye seek, shall suddenly come to his temple, even the messenger of the covenant, whom ye delight in: behold, he shall come, saith the Lord of hosts" (Malachi 3:1).

However, this prophecy may have more than one fulfillment. Elder Bruce R. McConkie pointed out that "the Lord, whom we seek, shall suddenly come to his temple, meaning that he will come to the earth, which is his temple, and also that he will come to those holy houses which he has commanded us to build unto his blessed name. Indeed, he came suddenly to the Kirtland Temple on the 3rd day of April in 1836; he has also appeared in others of his holy houses; and he will come in due course to the temples in Jackson County and in Jerusalem. And he will come to his American Zion and his Jewish Jerusalem."[116]

Clearly, we must leave the door open that, although the Savior will return to a temple to be built in Independence, Jackson County, Missouri, such a temple is not the only house of the Lord to which Christ will come. Thus, there is no need for inappropriate zealousness to gather to that area in anticipation of His return. Stakes of Zion are essential to the spiritual health and vigor of the center place. The center of Zion is no more holy than the other "holy places" designated as stakes by the hand of the Lord (see D&C 101:17–23).

It was never intended that all of the Saints take up their sickle to harvest the singular spot of Zion's center place. Fewer than two decades after the first pioneers arrived in the Great Salt Lake Valley, the Saints were concerned about the efforts they were expending if they were to leave it behind to gather to Missouri. President Brigham Young responded, "Remarks have been made as to our staying here [in the Rockies]. I will tell you how long we shall stay here. If we live our religion, we shall stay here in these mountains forever and forever, worlds without end, and a portion of the Priesthood will go and redeem and build up the centre Stake of Zion."[117]

Zion is to extend the width and breadth of the earth, with stakes established and temples built. These temples may well become the meeting places of the Saints and Christ throughout the world as referred to in revelation that the Lord will stand "upon the mighty ocean, even the great deep, and upon the islands of the sea, and upon the land of Zion" (D&C 133:20).

One Hundred and Forty-Four Thousand

The revelation that 144,000 will accompany the Savior in His appearance on Mount Zion gives some indication as to purposes of these private appearances to the Saints. John heard an angel declare to four other angels that during the time of the sixth seal—the era of the Restoration of the fulness of the gospel—they were to "have sealed the servants of our God in their foreheads" (Revelation 7:3). The number of those sealed was 144,000—12,000 from each of the tribes of Israel. The seal upon this group was the written name of the Father (see Revelation 14:1; D&C 133:18). The Prophet Joseph Smith explained that "where it says and they shall seal the servants of God in their foreheads &c it means to seal the blessing on their heads meaning the new and everlasting covenant thereby making their calling & election sure."[118] The Prophet further clarified that this is "the covenant of Abraham," whereby an individual "is sealed unto the throne, & the doctrine of Election sealing the father & children together."[119] Joseph further emphasized "the necessity of the Temple that the Servants of God may be sealed in their foreheads."[120] The 144,000 are the "priests and kings" described by the Prophet Joseph Smith and Sidney Rigdon in their account of the vision of celestial glory (D&C 76:56). Elder Bruce R. McConkie explained that they have been "converted, baptized, endowed, married for eternity, and finally sealed up unto eternal life."[121]

"What are we to understand by the sealing of the hundred and forty-four thousand?" (D&C 77:11) the Prophet Joseph Smith asked. He then received the following explanation: "We are to understand that those who are sealed are high priests, ordained unto the holy order of God, to administer the everlasting gospel; for they are they who are ordained out of every nation, kindred, tongue, and people, by the angels to whom is given power over the nations of the earth, to bring as many as will come to the church of the Firstborn" (D&C 77:11).

Curiously, in this explanation, the Prophet did not dwell on the number *144,000* as an absolute quantity. The book of Revelation is highly symbolic and often utilizes numbers that convey figurative meaning. For example, there are seven angels sounding seven trumps (see Revelation 8:2) or pouring out the wrath of God from seven vials (Revelation 15:7). A wicked man is given the number *666* (see Revelation 13:18). Reference to 144,000 may have more to do with quality of priesthood authority than it does with the quantity of priesthood holders. In other words, to be one of the 144,000 is a symbolic description referring to the authority these high priests have rather than saying there are exactly 144,000 priesthood holders. Similarly, we refer to an individual Apostle as a member of the *Twelve*. If members of the *Twelve* die, the remaining Apostles do not become members of the *Ten* or of the *Eleven* but are still referred to as members of the *Twelve*. This membership as one of the *Twelve* says more about the apostolic authority of the individual than emphasizing the number in the quorum. Likewise, to refer to an individual as a *Seventy* does not place emphasis on the number of the maximum members that can belong to the quorum but rather places emphasis on an office in the priesthood that is named *Seventy*, similar to the office of elder or high priest, etc.[122]

Therefore, to be a member of the 144,000 may indicate the authority and responsibility given to these high priests. Richard Draper explained, "Twelve represents the priesthood. Biblical people squared a number to amplify its symbolic meaning. Thus, 144 suggests a fullness of priesthood authority. . . . [John] gives the image a superlative quality by multiplying 1,000, representing completeness."[123] The Lord referred to the authority to administer temple ordinances for the living and the dead as "the fulness of the priesthood" (D&C 124:28).

Regarding the association of high priests, temple work on Mount Zion, and the Church of the Firstborn, we know that those inheriting celestial glory are high priests or "priests of the Most High, after the order of Melchizedek" (D&C 76:57). Further, the twelve tribes of Israel have been "scattered upon all the face of the earth, and also among all nations" (1 Nephi 22:3). The gathering of Israel through the Restoration of the gospel includes Saints of every nation. Temple blessings will be administered to these Saints by those of their own nation and in their own tongue (see Revelation 5:9–10; D&C 90:11).

Confirmed members of The Church of Jesus Christ of Latter-day Saints have been baptized and have received the gift of the Holy Ghost. Members of the Church of the Firstborn have received, in addition to these ordinances, all of the ordinances of the house of the Lord. They have entered into the new and everlasting covenant of marriage, and this covenant has been "sealed unto them by the Holy Spirit of Promise" (D&C 132:19). Thus, they are "sealed up unto eternal life . . . through the power of the Holy Priesthood" (D&C 131:5), and it is apparent that the 144,000 high priests are set apart to play a part in perfecting the Saints and administering the highest ordinances of the house of the Lord, bringing "as many as will come to the church of the Firstborn" (D&C 77:11). "It is not only necessary that you should be baptized for your dead," the Prophet Joseph Smith taught, "but you will have to go through all the ordinances for them, the same as you have gone through to save yourselves. There will be 144,000 saviors on Mount Zion, and with them an innumerable host that no man can number. Oh! I beseech you to go forward, go forward and make your calling and your election sure."[124] The Lord explained in revelation that "they who are the church of the Firstborn . . . are priests and kings . . . who overcome by faith, and are sealed by the Holy Spirit of Promise" (D&C 76:53–54, 56).

Everything that has been revealed leads us to the conclusion that the Savior will appear with 144,000 on Mount Zion to usher in the ever-important administration of the fullness of blessings in temples during the millennial era. Indeed, the Millennium is the great era of preparing for exaltation, including the fullness of temple ordinances. Surely, there will be need for those who have received the highest ordinances of salvation to administer these same ordinances for the living and the dead. In addition, for such to be the case, each high priest would be accompanied by his eternal companion in administering and receiving these ordinances in behalf of the dead. It is altogether proper that a veil be drawn over the meanings of all temple work alluded to. They appropriately belong to the houses of the Lord and may be understood by those who worthily enter therein, if not at the present, then in that future day when Christ comes to His temples.

Appearances to the Saints: Caught Up to Meet Christ in the Clouds

The Savior promised that His Saints would return to the earth with Him "when he shall come in the clouds of heaven to reign on the earth over his people" (D&C 76:63). Two groups of people are included with those whom the Savior will bring with Him in the clouds of heaven. First, "the saints that are upon the earth, who are alive, shall be quickened and caught up to meet him" (D&C 88:96). Second, lest any believe that the living will have priority over the dead to return with the Savior, the Apostle Paul clarified that those who are dead will be redeemed from the grave and also be caught up to meet the Savior. "They who are alive at the coming of the Lord, shall not prevent them who remain unto the coming of the Lord, who are asleep," Paul wrote to the Saints in Thessalonica. "For the Lord himself shall descend from heaven with a shout, with the voice of the archangel, and with the trump of God: and the dead in Christ shall rise first: Then they who are alive, shall be caught up together into the clouds with them who remain, to meet the Lord in the air" (JST, 1 Thessalonians 4:15–17; see also D&C 88:97–98).

In His Olivet Discourse, the Savior referred to a separation of the wicked and the righteous. "Then shall be fulfilled that which is written,"

He taught, "that in the last days, two shall be in the field, the one shall be taken, and the other left; two shall be grinding at the mill, the one shall be taken, and the other left" (Joseph Smith—Matthew 1:44).

Possibly, because of the similarities between the wording of the passages in the Bible and those in the scriptures of the Restoration, some Saints have momentarily applied an evangelical biblical interpretation and terminology to this event—the *Rapture*. Various creative works of art depict the righteous being caught from the earth and saved from the destructions that attend the time of the Second Coming. These ideas may give the false impression that the righteous will not be subject to the tribulations of the last days. Thus, it may be beneficial to clarify that which has been revealed.

First, no term to describe the prophesied lifting up from the earth and quickening of the righteous has been given in Restoration scriptures. Second, the Lord explained that the Saints who are to be caught up to be with the Savior do not join with the Lord in the clouds of heaven before many of the prophesied destructions that are to precede the Savior's appearances. Incidences of wars, famines, earthquakes, holocausts, hurricanes, tornadoes, and more have already repeatedly affirmed that both the righteous and the wicked are subject together to the attendant destructions. In each occasion, although there may have been divine guidance or protection, there has been no rapture from the earth to spare the righteous. Rather, the Lord has repeatedly referred to Zion and her stakes as "a land of peace, a city of refuge, a place of safety for the saints of the Most High God" (D&C 45:66). The great cleansing of the earth as if by fire will not destroy the righteous. On the other hand, the Lord revealed that the wicked will be destroyed at His coming, which will be discussed further in the chapter on the Savior's appearances to the world.

Unlike the Savior's private appearances to the Saints at Adam-ondi-Ahman and Mount Zion, no specific earthly locations are associated with this event or events. Rather, the scriptural explanations speak of the Saints being caught up from the earth, wherever they may be, to meet Christ in the clouds of heaven. If any event associated with the Second Coming wants for further revelation and explanation, this does.

It may appear a bit hard to comprehend thousands and millions caught up into the heavens. Being caught up into the clouds of heaven to meet the Savior may be a similar event to the city of Enoch—Zion. That city "was taken up into heaven" (Moses 7:23). In addition, others "were caught up by the powers of heaven into Zion" (Moses 7:27). Among those who were later taken into the heavens were the people of Melchizedek (JST, Genesis 14:34). Others are mentioned individually as having been taken into heaven or translated, such as Moses, Elijah, John the Revelator, and the three Nephites. Thus, although not a common occurrence in the last days, such a momentous event is not foreign to mortals throughout the history of the earth.

11
CHRIST'S APPEARANCE TO THE JEWISH REMNANT GATHERED AT JERUSALEM

FOR NEARLY TWO THOUSAND YEARS, the chair reserved for the children of Judah at the Lord's table has been empty, and lasting peace and brotherly love among those living in the holy city of Jerusalem have been but a hope. In time, the Jewish remnant of the house of Israel will return to the covenant made with Abraham, Isaac, and Jacob. Consequently, Jerusalem will truly be a holy city in deed as well as in multiplication of religious sites.

The gospel of Jesus Christ has the power to soften hardened hearts. In the latter days, the restored gospel first went to the Gentile nations. However, the Lord mandated that the day would come in which He would gather the Jewish remnant and they also would be taught the fulness of the gospel (see Isaiah 11:11–12; 3 Nephi 20:29–31; D&C 45:24–25). The foretold conversion of the Jewish remnant will be nothing short of miraculous. The Messiah for whom they wait with great anticipation will appear to them on the Mount of Olives, east of the city of old Jerusalem. At that time, they will learn that Jesus of Nazareth, whom their fathers rejected, is the true Messiah. He will redeem them from the false traditions of their fathers, and a nation will be converted to Christ in a day (Isaiah 66:5–13). The long day of dispersion and wandering will end, and the Jewish remnant will join with other descendants of Israel in building the millennial kingdom of God.

Since the time that the mortal Messiah walked among them, the story of the Jewish remnant has been one of desolation, destruction, and dispersion. During the last week of the Savior's life, while seated on the Mount of Olives, He taught His disciples, "Desolation shall come upon this generation as a thief in the night, and this people shall be destroyed and scattered among all nations." He further prophesied, "And this temple which ye now see shall be thrown down that there shall not be left one stone upon another" (D&C 45:19–20). A Roman army under the direction of Titus destroyed the city of Jerusalem in AD 70, and the temple was burned and dismantled stone by stone. The huge ashlars were pushed over the edge of the retaining wall onto the stone-paved streets below, and the temple mount was left in a heap of rubble. Today, many of these stones have been discovered by archaeologists uncovering the ancient road that runs beneath the southwest corner of the temple mount. The stones themselves symbolize the history of the Jews because similar to the temple buildings from which the stones were taken, the Jewish remnant has been destroyed and scattered upon Gentile roads. The fulness of the gospel that they rejected was taken from among them and given to the Gentile nations.

After the Jews' beloved Jerusalem was spoiled and left in ashes, it was rebuilt as a Roman city. At one time, following a failed Jewish uprising, the Roman rulers banned all Jews from entering the city; thus, Gentiles controlled the city for nearly two thousand years. Various foreign overlords each had their day to sway the scepter of power. Over the centuries that followed, the citizens of Judah were scattered throughout the world and continually looked forward to the next year in Jerusalem.

The Return of the Jewish Remnant to Jerusalem and the Building of the Temple

With an eye on the latter days, the Savior spoke of conditions among the Jewish remnant that would exist preceding His return in glory, when Jerusalem would no longer "be trodden down of the Gentiles" (Luke 21:24). "Judah must return," the Prophet Joseph Smith explained, "Jerusalem must be rebuilt, and the temple, and water come out from under the temple, and the waters of the Dead Sea be healed. It will take some time to rebuild the walls of the city and the temple, &c.; and all this must be done before the Son of Man will make His appearance."[125]

Latter-day Saints have shown considerable interest and entertained speculation regarding the building of the Jerusalem temple. Some have assumed that the temple must be built on the same location as Herod's temple, where today the holy Muslim Mosque of Omar, known as the Dome of the Rock, is located. Obviously, such a course would bring the conflict between the Jews and the Muslims to a climactic head. Thus, in this scenario, the temple is associated with devastating war and destruction between those two peoples and their allies or concerned nations. I grant that the prophecies do not preclude such a fulfillment. However, neither do they specify that the temple must occupy that space and only that space.

In a similar vein, it is not clear whether the temple will be built before the Savior's appearance to the Jewish remnant or after that appearance, but we do know it must happen before His grand appearance to the world. The Prophet Ezekiel placed his vision of the future Jerusalem temple following several significant events. These events include the destruction of Gog and his armies, seven years of burning weapons of war, seven months of burying the dead, and the great feast in which the beasts and fowls of the air devour the flesh of those destroyed (see Ezekiel 39; D&C 29:9–20). Reasonably, those who have been converted to the restored gospel of Jesus Christ will build this temple. Indeed, the Lord ordained Jerusalem as a place of refuge and as one of the places for baptisms for the dead (see D&C 124:36). If the prophesied temple is built before the Savior's appearance to the Jewish remnant on the Mount of Olives and if it is built by the members of Christ's restored Church, our understandings must expand to include a tremendous change in Jerusalem in which The Church of Jesus Christ of Latter-day Saints plays a prominent part in that pre-Second Coming story. If, on the other hand, the prophesied temple will be built by those of the Jewish remnant to whom the Savior will appear on the Mount of Olives but is done before Christ's appearance to the world, it may be that Latter-day Saints will have a greater part to play after the Olivet appearance than previous to it. Either way, we do know that like the rebuilding of the city of Jerusalem and the temple as its crowning jewel, the Jewish remnant is to be gathered and eventually blessed with the priesthood and the fulness of the gospel.

In the dedicatory prayer for the Kirtland Temple, the Prophet Joseph Smith was inspired to request of the Lord, "Thou knowest that thou has a great love for the children of Jacob, who have been scattered upon the mountains for a long time, in a cloudy and dark day. We therefore ask thee to have mercy upon the children of Jacob, that Jerusalem, from this hour, may begin to be redeemed; and the yoke of bondage may begin to be broken off from the house of David; and the children of Judah may begin to return to the lands which thou didst give to Abraham, their father" (D&C 109:61–64).

The Prophet Joseph Smith commissioned Elder Orson Hyde to travel to the land of Palestine and specifically to Jerusalem. Elder Hyde's mission was to dedicate the ancient biblical land and city for the return of a Jewish remnant. On Sunday morning, October 24, 1841, a good while before day, Elder Hyde crossed from the city to the Mount of Olives. In the dedicatory prayer he offered, he consecrated the "land for three primary objectives: the gathering of Judah, the building up of Jerusalem, and the rearing of a Temple. The remainder of the prayer was for the most part a supplication for blessings to accomplish those three objectives."[126]

The miracle of the rebuilding of Jerusalem by the Jews has happened under the watchful eye of the Almighty. Since the morning that Elder Orson Hyde knelt on the Mount of Olives and fulfilled his assignment, Jews have been stirred up in spirit to return to the land of their forefathers. This is not to say that the Lord condones the bloodshed or the confiscation of property that has occurred in the Jewish redemption of the land of Palestine. Applicable to the Jewish nation are the words of the Lord to the Saints concerning the establishment of Zion in Jackson County, Missouri: "Wherefore, the land of Zion shall not be obtained but by purchase or by blood, otherwise there is none inheritance for you. And if by purchase, behold you are blessed; and if by blood, as you are forbidden to shed blood, lo, your enemies are upon you, and ye shall be scourged from synagogue to synagogue, and but few shall stand to receive an inheritance" (D&C 63:29–31). The events cited have transpired over a number of years. There are yet more to take place.

The Fulness of the Gospel to Be Taught to the Jewish Remnant

In fulfillment of ancient prophecy and modern inspired prayers, the gathering of the Jews to Jerusalem is one of the most easily identifiable signs of the times. This gathering signals the fulfillment of the *times of the Gentiles*, the present era in which we live. The gathering to Jerusalem foreshadows the period in which the *times of the Jews* will begin—"That is," Elder Bruce R. McConkie wrote, "the era will commence in which the Jews shall accept the gospel and be blessed spiritually in an abundant way."[127]

The Lord indicated that in the latter days the restored gospel is to "go forth unto the ends of the earth, unto the Gentiles first, and then, behold, and lo, they shall turn unto the Jews" (D&C 90:9). The Second Coming ushers in the time when the Jewish nation will once again receive opportunity to hear the gospel and enter into the covenant of God. When the fulness of the gospel can go to the Jews instead of only to the Gentile nations, it may be said that the times of the Gentiles is fulfilled, but before that change occurs, the Savior prophesied that the Jews will again gather in preparation to receive their King. As previously mentioned, Luke's account of the Olivet Discourse indicates that "Jerusalem shall be trodden down of the Gentiles, until the times of the Gentiles be fulfilled" (Luke 21:24). After centuries of non-Jewish domination of the holy city, war brought Jerusalem under Jewish control in 1967. The Six-Day War, which began June 5, was a turning point in history. The holy city was annexed, and shortly thereafter, the state of Israel declared Jerusalem to be its capitol.

The Prophet Nephi foretold the time in which "the Jews which are scattered also shall begin to believe in Christ; and they shall begin to gather in upon the face of the land" (2 Nephi 30:7). Elder Bruce R. McConkie clarified, "The Jews 'shall begin to believe in Christ' before he comes the second time. Some of them will accept the gospel and forsake the traditions of their fathers; a few will find in Jesus the fulfillment of their ancient Messianic hopes; but their nation as a whole, their people as the distinct body that they now are in all nations, the Jews as a unit shall not, at that time, accept the word of truth. But a beginning will be made; a foundation will be laid; and then Christ will come and usher in the millennial year of his redeemed."[128]

It appears, from Nephi's prophecy, that the gospel will first be taught to the scattered Jews. In other words, the first Jews to accept the gospel will not be those in Jerusalem or their ancient homeland in Palestine. Rather, those living in Gentile nations will be baptized and gathered to Christ and His restored Church.

Who shall teach those Jews gathered to Jerusalem of the Messiah whom their fathers rejected? Before the Lord returns, He will raise up two special witnesses to the Jewish remnant of Jerusalem: "They are two prophets that are to be raised up to the Jewish nation in the last days, at the time of the restoration, and to prophesy to the Jews after they are gathered and have built the city of Jerusalem in the land of their fathers" (D&C 77:15).

Their ministry is of great importance in the Lord's plan to redeem His people from the centuries of spiritual darkness that have entrapped them and to prepare for His return. After nearly two millennia of no prophetic word, voices of God's prophets will once again be raised to the children of Judah in Jerusalem. These prophets will come with authority to baptize for the remission of sins, as did John the Baptist in preparing the way for the first coming of Christ. As Zechariah expressed it, "In that day there shall be a fountain opened to the house of David and to the inhabitants of Jerusalem for sin and uncleanness" (Zechariah 13:1). The authority restored to the Prophet Joseph Smith to perform priesthood ordinances will bless the lives of those who accept Jesus of Nazareth as the Son of God. It seems logical that these prophets will teach the gathered remnant of the Book of Mormon, written to "the convincing of the Jew and Gentile that Jesus is the Christ, the Eternal God" (Title Page of the Book of Mormon) and that the words of the book will be like a voice from the dust to them. How many will accept the message of the Restoration is unknown, but the word will go forth like that of John of old in preparing the people to receive their Messiah when He appears to them.[129]

The length of the two prophets' ministry among the Jews has been revealed in symbolic, if not also literal, terms. An angel informed John that "they shall prophesy a thousand two hundred and threescore days [1,260 days, or three and a half years] clothed in sackcloth" (Revelation 11:3). The common symbol of three and a half in the book of Revelation indicates that their ministry will occur during a time of Satan's power on the earth, as it is consistently symbolic of the period in which evil dominates the mortal plain. The mere mention of the two foretold prophets who will raise their voices in Jerusalem has the potential to evoke great speculation. Elder Bruce R. McConkie suggested that the description of the power to shut heaven and to smite the earth with plagues at their word points to these two witnesses being members of the First Presidency or the Quorum of the Twelve Apostles.[130] He reasoned that members of these two quorums are given the sealing keys and are those who might be sent by the Lord to fulfill His purposes in the city, "which spiritually is called Sodom and Egypt, where also our Lord was crucified" (Revelation 11:8). As a result, Saints pay rapt attention to any mention of Apostles or members of the First Presidency who travel to the Holy Land. The general assumption is that according to the timetable given in the Apostle John's revelation, once the two prophets commence their ministry in Jerusalem, there are yet three and a half years before the Savior will return to the earth in glory. What such reasoning fails to acknowledge is that the number is symbolic and that the Savior's appearance to the Saints and their day of judgment may very well precede the ministry of these two prophets.

The inhabitants of Jerusalem as a whole will not receive the witness of these two prophets. During the three and a half years of their ministry, the prophets will be protected by divine power. "And if any man will hurt them, fire proceedeth out of their mouth, and devoureth their enemies: and if any man will hurt them, he must in this manner be killed" (Revelation 11:5). Such authority is a powerful reminder for the people of the book—the keepers of the sacred records of the Old Testament prophets—that God's servants walk among them again, akin to the revered prophet Elijah, who sealed the heavens and called on God to send down fire as a witness that the Lord is God and that he was God's servant (see 1 Kings 17:1; 18:36–38).

But this is not all. The power exercised by these two prophets "over waters to turn them to blood, and to smite the earth with all plagues, as often as they will" (Revelation 11:5) will give to the Jewish remnant the same witness Moses provided Pharaoh and the Egyptians. How could even the blind fail to see that these men will be sent from the God of Abraham, Isaac, and Jacob? How could the deaf fail to hear the Spirit testify that they speak the words of life? Yet, "when they shall have finished their testimony, the beast that ascendeth out of the bottomless pit shall make war against them, and shall overcome them, and kill them" (Revelation 11:7). "Satan shall slay them, by the hands of those in his employ, even as he slew the Lord and the prophets who were before them."[131] The Apostle John was informed that the wicked will cause the unburied bodies of these special witnesses to lie in the street in Jerusalem as evidence of their enemies' evil triumph. They will "rejoice over them, and make merry, and shall send gifts one to another; because these two prophets tormented them that dwelt on the earth" (Revelation 11:10). At the end of three and a half days, the rejoicing of the wicked will cease and great fear will enter their hearts because to their wonder and amazement, God's servants will stand upon their feet and ascend into heaven while their enemies gaze in horror. However, as the Savior explained in the parable of the beggar Lazarus and the rich man, "If they hear not Moses and the prophets, neither will they be persuaded, though one rose from the dead" (Luke 16:31). The day of their wickedness is about to come to an abrupt end.

Christ Will Appear to the Jewish Remnant

During the time God's two special witnesses are ministering or sometime thereafter, there will be many who dwell in Jerusalem who shall look for their Messiah to return (see D&C 45:43–44). It will be a time of great worldwide tribulation, but more especially in Palestine and Jerusalem.

The prophet Zechariah recorded the word of the Lord foretelling that at the time of the Jewish gathering, all nations of the earth would take interest in Jerusalem. This prophecy reads like the headlines of modern news media: the conflicting political situations and claims to land in Palestine complicate peaceful resolutions. In addition, all foreign nations that have sought to govern Jerusalem have had to deal with the religious devotion associated with sacred sites for three great religious faiths of the world—Jewish, Christian, and Muslim—and such has proven to be greater than their ability to manage. In greater measure than it has before, at a future day, Jerusalem will demand the attention of the entire world. It will become "a cup of trembling" and a "burdensome stone for all people: all that burden themselves with it shall be cut in pieces, though all the people of the earth be gathered together against it" (Zechariah 12:2–3). Sadly, such warnings give no hope that weary ambassadors and political conferences will bring lasting agreements and peace to Jerusalem and its people. Indeed, it seems that just the opposite will be the case until Christ ushers in the millennial reign of peace.

The Lord spoke of a time when He would destroy the nations of the world that will be in siege against both Judah—the latter-day Jewish remnant—and the city of Jerusalem (see Zechariah 12:2–3, 9). He declared that the enigmatic Gog will come from the north parts with a mighty army "against my people of Israel, as a cloud to cover the land; it shall be in the latter days, and I will bring thee against my land, that the heathen may know me, when I shall be sanctified in thee, O Gog, before their eyes" (Ezekiel 38:16). The Apostle John referred to the gathering of the world's armies, specifically among the kings of the east, as "the battle of that great day of God Almighty . . . And he gathered them together into a place called in the Hebrew tongue Armageddon" (Revelation 16:14, 16).

Apparently, near the time of Armageddon, misery and destruction will once again visit Jerusalem. Jesus spoke of this as the time when abomination would again bring desolation to Jerusalem as spoken of by Daniel the prophet (see Joseph Smith—Matthew 1:12, 32). "And it shall come to pass, that in all the land, saith the Lord, two parts therein shall be cut off and die; but the third part shall be left therein. And I will bring the third part through the fire, and will refine them as silver is refined, and will try them as gold is tried: they shall call on my name, and I will hear them: I will say, It is my people: and they shall say, The Lord is my God" (Zechariah 13:8–9). In His wisdom, the Lord knows how to best overcome centuries of tradition and persecution as

He softens the hearts of His people. In time, the Jewish remnant will receive the true Messiah. The trials of battle will reach into the homes of those at Jerusalem "and the city shall be taken, and the houses rifled, and the women ravished; and half of the city shall go into captivity" (Zechariah 14:2).

The Lord of hosts will deliver His people, and His arm shall fall upon the nations: "Then shall the Lord go forth, and fight against those nations, as when he fought in the day of battle . . . And this shall be the plague wherewith the Lord will smite all the people that have fought against Jerusalem; Their flesh shall consume away while they stand upon their feet, and their eyes shall consume away in their holes, and their tongue shall consume away in their mouth" (Zechariah 14:3, 12). The prophet Ezekiel referred to this same destruction. Referring to Gog and his armies, the Lord revealed to Ezekiel, "I will plead against him with pestilence and with blood; and I will rain upon him, and upon his bands, and upon the many people that are with him, an overflowing rain, and great hailstones, fire, and brimstone. Thus will I magnify myself, and sanctify myself; and I will be known in the eyes of many nations, and they shall know that I am the Lord" (Ezekiel 38:22–23).

We are indebted to the Lord for revealing to the prophet Zechariah the greater part of the knowledge available to us concerning the circumstances attending Christ's appearance in Jerusalem. Thankfully, we may also add to Zechariah's revelations those given to the Prophet Joseph Smith concerning the event of the actual appearance. Regarding those in Jerusalem, the Lord revealed, "And the remnant shall be gathered to this place; and then they shall look for me, and, behold, I will come; and they shall see me in the clouds of heaven, clothed with power and great glory; and with all the holy angels" (D&C 45:43–44). More specifically, "His feet shall stand in that day upon the mount of Olives, which is before Jerusalem on the east . . . and it shall cleave in twain, and the earth shall tremble, and reel to and fro, and the heavens also shall shake. . . . And the mount of Olives shall cleave in the midst thereof toward the east and toward the west, and there shall be a very great valley; and half of the mountain shall remove toward the north, and half of it toward the south" (Zechariah 14:4; D&C 45:48). The Jews will "flee to the valley of the mountains" (Zechariah 14:5).

The Jewish remnant shall finally see the Messiah's promised day of deliverance for which they have waited century upon century to come, a day when their Savior will conquer their enemies. We anticipate that love, exultation, and awe will fill their bosoms as they gaze upon Him who is mighty to save. Then, in confusion, they will note that their Messiah carries unexpected wounds. His hands and feet will be pierced. With their eyes fixed upon their Deliverer, they will ask him, "What are these wounds in thine hands and in thy feet" (D&C 45:51)? Consequently, they shall be taught the truth concerning their Messiah's identity as He will answer them, "These wounds are the wounds with which I was wounded in the house of my friends. I am he who was lifted up. I am Jesus that was crucified. I am the Son of God" (D&C 45:52). Great sorrow will sweep over them as they weep for their iniquities, and they shall "lament because they persecuted their king" (D&C 45:53).

The Lord revealed to Zechariah that mercifully "I will pour upon the house of David, and upon the inhabitants of Jerusalem, the spirit of grace and of supplications: and they shall look upon me whom they have pierced, and they shall mourn for him, as one mourneth for his only son, and shall be in bitterness for him, as one that is in bitterness for his firstborn. In that day shall there be a great mourning in Jerusalem" (Zechariah 12:10–11). Jacob testified, "The Messiah will set himself again the second time to recover them; wherefore, he will manifest himself unto them in power and great glory, unto the destruction of their enemies, when that day cometh when they shall believe in him" (2 Nephi 6:14). Thus, Jesus Christ, the Son of God, shall reclaim the Jewish remnant. The Mount of Olives, its western slope once home to Gethsemane and the site of the Savior's agony, shall become the site of His return in glory. Those individuals whose fathers once rejected their Messiah will then receive Him in repentant humility. A nation that has wandered in spiritual darkness for centuries will then be converted to "the true Messiah, who was rejected by them" (2 Nephi 25:15–18; see also 1 Nephi 10:14). Sorrow for sin and rejoicing for deliverance shall again be heard in Jerusalem. Israel will be united. The Lord declared that He will make Judah and Joseph "one nation in the land upon the mountains of Israel; and one king shall be king to them all: and they shall be no more two nations . . . Neither shall they defile themselves any more. . . . but I will save them out of all their dwellingplaces, wherein they have sinned, and will cleanse them: so shall they be my people, and I will be their God" (Ezekiel 37:22–23).

At some time, apparently after He appears on the Mount of Olives, Christ will enter the Jerusalem Temple Mount through the gate that faces east, toward Olivet. In vision of a future temple in Jerusalem, Ezekiel saw "the gate of the outward sanctuary which looketh toward the east; and it was shut. Then said the Lord unto me: This gate shall be shut, it shall not be opened, and no man shall enter in by it; because the Lord, the God of Israel, hath entered in by it, therefore it shall be shut" (see Ezekiel 44:1–2). Today that gate, the only gate providing direct access to the Temple Mount from outside the city, is blocked by stone filling the entryway. Much of the present-day wall and gates of Jerusalem's Old City were rebuilt in the sixteenth century during the reign of the Ottoman sultan, Suleiman the Magnificent. The gate that led to the Temple Mount faced the east anciently and was called the Golden Gate. Today, that ancient gate from biblical times is assumed to be buried beneath centuries of rubble. One view is that the modern eastern gate, which has been walled up since the sixteenth century, is built directly over that ancient biblical gate. "A traditional tale relates that Suleiman feared a Christian [or Jewish] Messiah would try to enter through the Golden Gate so he had it blocked up."[132] Reportedly, others believe that the Muslim cemetery occupying the land in front of the gate blocks the entrance to the gate with the assumption that the Jewish Messiah would not risk being defiled by walking on a burial ground. The traditions illustrate the conflict between the Muslims and the Jews in claiming the Temple Mount. Muslims refer to it as the mount of Haram esh-Sharif, the Noble Sanctuary, upon which stands two sacred structures, the Dome of the Rock and Al Aksa Mosque. Although the blocked gate leading to the Temple Mount is of more modern construction, its location and the legends associated with it serve to make it a point of religious and political sensitivity. A group of Jews who anticipate the day in which they will reclaim the holy mount and build a temple adds to the sensitivity and interest in the Golden Gate. A webcam has been set up and is focused on the eastern wall—the Messiah Cam—hoping to broadcast the Messiah entering the Temple Mount through the Golden Gate.

While they wait to capture that moment, we too await further word from the Lord to know whether the temple in Jerusalem will be built before the Savior's appearance to the Jews or whether the very Jewish remnant who witnesses His Olivet appearance in glory will build that temple.

12
APPEARANCE TO THE
RIGHTEOUS IN THE WORLD
AND THE DESTRUCTION OF
THE WICKED OF THE WORLD

THE SCRIPTURES ALLUDE TO A separate appearance to the world but also seem to indicate that the appearance on the Mount of Olives is associated with the appearance to the world. Review the description that the Savior gave of His appearance on the Mount of Olives:

> And the [Jewish] remnant shall be gathered unto this place [Mount Olivet/Jerusalem] and then they [the Jewish remnant] shall look for me, and, behold, I will come; and they shall see me in the clouds of heaven, clothed with power and great glory; with all the holy angels. . . . Then shall the Lord set his foot upon this mount [the Mount of Olives]. . . . And the Lord shall utter his voice, and *all the ends of the earth* shall hear it; and *the nations of the earth* shall mourn. . . . And they that have watched for iniquity shall be hewn down and cast into the fire. And then shall the Jews look upon me and say: What are these wounds in thine hands and in thy feet? . . . Then shall the heathen nations be redeemed, and they that knew no law shall have part in the first resurrection. (D&C 45:43–54; emphasis added)

The prophesied events that will lead up to the Savior's appearance on the Mount of Olives recorded in the forty-fifth section of the Doctrine and Covenants mention only His appearance to the world in the Joseph Smith Translation of that same discourse. That account reads: "Then shall all the tribes of the earth mourn; and they shall see the Son of Man coming in the clouds of heaven, with power and great glory" (Joseph Smith—Matthew 1:36). I have taken the approach of understanding the general appearance to the world as distinct from the private appearances to the Saints or to the Jewish remnant. This is in harmony with President Ezra Taft Benson's description discussed in the introductory chapter on the Second Coming.

Somewhat surprisingly, even though Christ's appearance to the world may be more often referred to as *the Second Coming*, the scriptures hold relatively little specific information regarding the Savior's grand public appearance to the world. It may be that more is revealed regarding the private appearances of the Savior to the Saints because those involved in those events actually study the prophecies. The Lord reveals truth to those who seek it; whereas, among the world and the wicked, the revelations in the scriptures would not be of much benefit to them because they simply would not believe them even if they read them. The wicked of the last days reject Christ and the signs of His divinity, and from them is taken the greater knowledge (see Alma 12:9–11).

Even with the information we have been given, the chronology of the Savior's appearances is still unknown. The time markers are tentative. For example, consider the following attempt to determine the sequence of events and their association to each other. In the Apostle John's revelation on the Isle of Patmos, he recorded regarding the ascension into heaven of the two witnesses to the Jewish nation that "the same hour was there a great earthquake" (Revelation 11:13), possibly referring to the great earthquake that will divide the Mount of Olives at the Savior's return. Still, we are left to ask if the "hour" mentioned by John has any relationship to an hour of sixty minutes or if it is simply stating that it was near that same time. Further of note is that at that same time, an "angel sounded; and there were great voices in heaven, saying, The kingdoms of this world are become the kingdoms of our Lord, and of his Christ; and he shall reign for ever and ever" (Revelation 11:15). Again, this possibly refers to the previous discussion regarding the events attending the Savior's appearance at Adam-ondi-Ahman. If so, the inhabitants of the earth will yet have to witness lightnings, thunderings, earthquakes, and great hail (see Revelation 11:19).

As previously discussed, great wickedness is associated with the era in which Christ will make His appearances to those on the earth. Indeed, the Lord referred to this wickedness that covers the earth as abomination and to the wicked of the world as being reigned over by a great whore named "BABYLON THE GREAT, THE MOTHER OF HARLOTS AND ABOMINATIONS OF THE EARTH" (Revelation 17:5). Plagues, pestilence, earthquakes, hurricanes, and wars will decimate the habitations of the wicked to cleanse the earth of their iniquity in preparation for the Savior to usher in a thousand years of peace. Yet, the wicked will either refuse to consider or will not be aware of the nearness of Christ's coming in glory and their imminent destruction.

In a warning to the Saints, the Savior revealed, "Verily I say unto you, the coming of the Lord draweth nigh, and it overtaketh the world as a thief in the night—Therefore, gird up your loins, that you may be children of light, and that day shall not overtake you as a thief" (D&C 106:4–5). Further, as previously discussed, the Savior likened the circumstances surrounding His appearance to an earlier time: "But as it was in the days of Noah, so it shall be also at the coming of the Son of Man; for it shall be with them, as it was in the days which were before the flood; for until the day that Noah entered into the ark they were . . . marrying and giving in marriage; and knew not until the flood came, and took them away; so shall also the coming of the Son of Man be" (Joseph Smith—Matthew 1:41–43).

On the other hand, many others "shall be looking forth for the great day of the Lord to come, even for the signs of the coming of the Son of Man" (D&C 45:39). Even among those who are aware of the Savior's promised return and pre-appearance signs, "men's hearts shall fail them, and they shall say that Christ delayeth his coming until the end of the earth" (D&C 45:26).

The time prior to the Savior's appearance to the world shall be one of great death and destruction among the wicked. Nephi wrote that "the blood of that great and abominable church, which is the whore of all the earth, shall turn upon their own heads; for they shall war among themselves. . . . And all that fight against Zion shall be destroyed . . . for the day soon cometh that all the proud and they who do wickedly shall be as stubble; and the day cometh that they must be burned" (1 Nephi 22:13–15). For that reason, the Lord warned the Saints, "Go ye out from among the nations, even from Babylon, from the midst of wickedness, which is spiritual Babylon" (D&C 133:14). "Come out of her, my people, that ye be not partakers of her sins, and that ye receive not of her plagues" (Revelation 18:4).

Significantly, the Second Coming of the Savior will occur in stark contrast with His birth as a helpless babe in Bethlehem, where few physically saw His humble arrival. Quite the opposite, Jesus Christ will return to the earth with power and glory, much like the sun rising in the morning sky and coursing across the heavens. All living upon the earth will see His Second Coming. In addition, as the light of the sun continues to fall upon the earth in the course of a day, so will the light of the Lord's return have many hours of visitation. His light will shine forth on Mount Zion, or the city of New Jerusalem, the Mount of Olives, the islands of the sea, and upon the land of Zion until the whole earth has received the Son of God, their King (see D&C 133:18–20).

Not all of the earth's inhabitants will recognize the significance of the Savior coming in glory. Apparently, some heathen nations will not have the blessing of the writings of the ancient prophets nor the teachings of latter-day seers. They will ask, "Who is this that cometh down from God in heaven with dyed garments; yea, from the regions which are not known, clothed in his glorious apparel, traveling in the greatness of his strength" (D&C 133:46)? Their introduction to the Only Begotten Son of God will not include the babe born in Bethlehem but will consist of the returning righteous King who has destroyed His wicked enemies. "He shall say: I am he who spake in righteousness, mighty to save" (D&C 133:47). Isaiah's reference to this occurrence asked, "Who is this that cometh from Edom, with dyed garments from Bozrah" (Isaiah 63:1)? Edom was a land in the ancient Near East, with Bozrah as its capitol. It was also referred to as Idumea, which, like Babylon or Egypt, is a scriptural symbol for that which is unclean—the world (see D&C 1:36). This appearance, in which the Christ is represented as wearing blood-red-stained garments follows the Lord's day of visitation upon the wicked.

The symbolic representation of the destruction of the wicked at Christ's coming is that of treading upon grapes in a winepress or a wine vat. The winepress was usually a flat stone area, upon which the grapes were trampled to release their juices. "The juice flowed through shallow channels to a vat hewn at one end of the pressing ground."[133] From early biblical times, the juice has been referred to as "the blood of grapes" (Genesis 49:11), providing an apt sacramental symbol of the blood Christ shed for the sins of the world. But this symbolic reference to wine flowing in the winepress does not denote the blood of Christ. Rather, regarding the destruction of the wicked, the Master will announce, "I have trodden the wine-press alone, and have brought judgment upon all people; and none were with me; and I have trampled them in my fury, and I did tread upon them in mine anger, and their blood have I sprinkled upon my garments, and stained all my raiment; for this was the day of vengeance which was in my heart" (D&C 133:50–51).

In further allusion, the wine vat is symbolically filled with the wrath of God, ready to be poured out upon the heads of the wicked. In his revelation, John saw an angel with sickle in hand to "gather the clusters of the vine of the earth; for her grapes are fully ripe. And the angel thrust in his sickle into the earth, and gathered the vine of the earth, and cast it into the great winepress of the wrath of God. And the winepress was trodden without the city, and blood came out of the winepress" (Revelation 14:18–20). The wine was placed in "seven golden vials full of the wrath of God," representing seven plagues to be poured out upon the heads of the wicked (Revelation 15:6–7).

The word picture is not a pretty one, but, then again, one should not expect the wrath of God to be pleasant. "Our heavenly Father is more liberal in His views, and boundless in His mercies and blessings, than we are ready to believe or receive," the Prophet Joseph Smith taught, "and, at the same time, is more terrible to the workers of iniquity, more awful in the executions of His punishments, and more ready to detect every false way, than we are apt to suppose Him to be."[134] The days of wickedness will come to a welcome end when the Savior tramples the offenders in His fury.

The destruction of the wicked may appear to be harsh and difficult to comprehend, but for a clearer understanding of Christ's love manifest in destroying the wicked, consider the outrage expressed when physical or sexual abuse of innocent victims is broadcast in the news media. Even greater is the indignation if it is also revealed that individuals knew of the ongoing abuse but did nothing to stop it. At times, the fury is overwhelming that anyone would stand idly by to allow innocent victims to suffer. After the long-suffering of His people, Christ will manifest His righteousness and love by symbolically trampling upon the wicked, removing them from ever again being able to heap sorrows upon the innocent. Lucifer has delighted in commanding human devils who have surrendered their wills to his hatred, but his power over men on earth will cease with "the end of the world, or the destruction of the wicked, which is the end of the world" (Joseph Smith—Matthew 1:4). The earth will be prepared for the millennial reign of peace, partly through the "fulness of the wrath of God [that] shall be poured out upon all the children of men; for he will not suffer that the wicked shall destroy the righteous" (1 Nephi 22:16).

John witnessed in vision and recorded the final episode of the last days and Second Coming of Christ: "And after these things I heard a great voice of much people in heaven, saying, Alleluia; Salvation, and glory, and honor, and power, unto the Lord our God: for true and righteous are his judgments." And again, "Alleluia: for the Lord God omnipotent reigneth. Let us be glad and rejoice, and give honor to him; for the marriage of the Lamb is come, and his wife hath made herself ready" (Revelation 19:1–2, 6–7). Those who remain upon the earth will "mention the loving kindness of their Lord, and all that he has bestowed upon them according to his goodness, and according to his loving kindness, forever and ever" (D&C 133:52).

With the Apostle John, let us heed the Savior's testimony, "Surely I come quickly. Amen," and echo John's feelings regarding the Second Coming of Christ, "Even so, come, Lord Jesus" (Revelation 22:20).

ENDNOTES

1. The revelation was received December 27–28, 1832, and January 3, 1833. See "Kirtland Council Minute Book," (np) 3–4; "Revelation Book 2," *The Joseph Smith Papers: Revelations and Translations; Manuscript Revelation Books,* eds. Robin Scott Jensen, Robert J. Woodruff, and Steven C. Harper, (Salt Lake City: The Church Historians Press, 2009), 479–507 (33–48 in the manuscript book).

2. Letter from Joseph Smith and John Whitmer to the Saints in Colesville, New York, Aug. 20, 1830, Harmony, Pennsylvania; in Newel Knight, Autobiography and Journal, ca. 1846–47, 133–36, Church Archives; Cited in *Teachings of Presidents of the Church: Joseph Smith,* (Salt Lake City: The Church of Jesus Christ of Latter-day Saints, 2007), 251–52.

3. David F. Holland, *Sacred Borders,* (New York City: Oxford University Press, 2011), 158.

4. "Seven or eight young men came to see me, part of them from the city of New York. They treated me with the greatest respect. I showed them the fallacy of Mr. Miller's data concerning the coming of Christ and the end of the world, or as it is commonly called, Millerism, and preached them quite a sermon; that error was in the Bible, or the translation of the Bible; that Miller was in want of correct information upon the subject, and that he was not so much to blame as the translators. I told them the prophecies must all be fulfilled; the sun must be darkened and the moon turned into blood, and many more things take place before Christ would come" (*History of The Church of Jesus Christ of Latter-day Saints,* 7 Vols. [Salt Lake City: Deseret Book Company, 1949], 5:271–72).

5. *Times and Seasons,* Vol. 2 No. 3, [December 1, 1840], 232.

6. *HC* 2:464.

7. *HC* 6:254. (At another time, the Prophet Joseph Smith explained, "The inhabitants of the earth are asleep: they know not the day of their visitation. The Lord hath set the bow in the cloud for a sign that while it shall be seen, seed time and harvest, summer and winter shall not fail; but when it shall disappear, woe to that generation, for behold the end cometh quickly" [*HC* 5:402]).

8. *HC* 5:336–337.

9. *The Words of Joseph Smith*, compiled and edited by Andrew F. Ehat and Lyndon W. Cook, (Provo, Utah: Religious Studies Center, Brigham Young University, 1980), 181.

10. *HC* 5:336

11. Ibid.

12. *Millennial Star*, 51:547; cited in *Discourses of Wilford Woodruff*, ed., G. Homer Durham, (Salt Lake City: Bookcraft, Inc., 1946, 1969), 255–256; emphasis added.

13. *Deseret Weekly*, Oct. 11, 1890, 517; cited in *Teachings of the Presidents of the Church: Wilford Woodruff*, (Salt Lake City: The Church of Jesus Christ of Latter-day Saints, 2004), 250.

14. *Millennial Star*, May 30, 1895, 355; cited in *Teachings of the Presidents of the Church: Wilford Woodruff*, (Salt Lake City: The Church of Jesus Christ of Latter-day Saints, 2004), 252.

15. *Messages of the First Presidency of the Church of Jesus Christ of Latter-day Saints*, vol. 4, James R. Clark, comp., (Salt Lake City: Bookcraft, Inc., 1970), 132.

16. Letter sent from the First Presidency, Wilford Woodruff, George Q. Cannon, and Joseph F. Smith, Salt Lake City, Utah, Sept. 7, 1897. *Messages of the First Presidency*, 6 vols., James R. Clark, comp., (Salt Lake City: Bookcraft, Inc., 1966), 3:287.

17. "The Rise and Decline of the LDS Indian Student Placement Program, 1947–1996," *Mormons, Scripture, and the Ancient World: Studies in Honor of John L. Sorenson*, ed. Davis Bitton, (Provo,

Utah: Foundation for Ancient Research and Mormon Studies at Brigham Young University, 1998), 92.

18. For example, see Bruce R. McConkie's *Doctrinal New Testament Commentary*, (Salt Lake City: Bookcraft, Inc., 1990), 3:501–503, 541–42.

19. Bruce R. McConkie, *Doctrinal New Testament Commentary*, (Salt Lake City: Bookcraft, Inc., 1976) 1:656.

20. "Closing Remarks," *Ensign*, Jan.1974, 125–26.

21. Ibid., 129.

22. "When the World Will Be Converted," *Ensign*, Oct. 1974, 5, 7.

23. "Admonitions for the Priesthood of God," *Ensign*, Jan. 1973.

24. Ibid; see also *The Improvement Era*, June 1970, 64.

25. See Bruce R. McConkie's *The Millennial Messiah*, (Salt Lake City: Deseret Book Company, 1983), 481.

26. *HC* 3:390; emphasis added.

27. Ibid.

28. *HC* 6:52.

29. *JD* 3:370.

30. *Deseret Weekly*, 53:642–43 (October 19, 1896); cited in *Discourses of Wilford Woodruff*, ed., G. Homer Durham, (Salt Lake City: Bookcraft, Inc., 1946, 1969), 288–89.

31. See Bruce R. McConkie's *The Millennial Messiah* and chapter summaries in the LDS edition of the King James Version of the Bible.

32. "When Shall These Things Be?" *Brigham Young University 1995–96 Speeches*, (Provo, Utah: Brigham Young University Publications and Graphics, 1996), 186.

33. *The Words of Joseph Smith*, compiled and edited by Andrew F. Ehat and Lyndon W. Cook, (Provo, Utah: Religious Studies Center, Brigham Young University, 1980), 181; punctuation standardized.

34. "Living in the Fulness of Times," *Ensign,* Nov. 2001, 6.

35. "Preparation for the Second Coming," *Ensign*, May 2004, 9.

36. My friend and colleague Richard D. Draper has written in detail regarding the conditions and causes of the fall of Jerusalem in AD 70. I acknowledge and appreciate his insights regarding the fall of Jerusalem. I recommend his volume *The Savior's Prophecies: From the Fall of Jerusalem to the Second Coming* to those who wish to have further reading on this topic.

37. *Church News*, 2 Feb. 1963, 16.

38. *The Savior's Prophecies: From the Fall of Jerusalem to the Second Coming,* (American Fork, Utah: Covenant Communications, Inc., 2001), 89.

39. Ibid., 95–96.

40. Josephus, *The Jewish War*, trans. G. A. Williamson, rev. E. Mary Smallwood, (London, England: Penguin Books Ltd., 1981), 278.

41. Ibid.

42. Ibid., 278–79.

43. "I Testify," *Ensign,* Nov. 1988, 87.

44. "The Times in Which We Live," *Ensign,* Nov. 2001, 72.

45. "Standing for Truth and Right," *Ensign*, Nov. 1997, 38.

46. *JD* 8:355–56.

47. *Gospel Doctrine*, (Salt Lake City, Utah: Deseret Book Company, 1986), 55.

48. "We Follow Jesus Christ," *Ensign*, May 2010, 85–86.

49. "First Presidency Statement on AIDS," *Ensign*, July 1988, 79.

50. *HC* 4:11.

51. *Adam Clarke's Commentary on the Bible*, abridged by Ralph Earl, (Grand Rapids, Michigan: Baker Book House, 1967), 1343.

52. *Opening the Seven Seals: The Visions of John the Revelator*, (Salt Lake City: Deseret Book Company, 1991), 96.

53. *CR*, Apr. 1995, 30.

54. "Tragedy or Destiny," *Faith Precedes the Miracle*, (Salt Lake City: Deseret Book Company, 1972), 96.

55. Ibid., 97.

56. The Prophet Joseph Smith taught, "At the first organization in heaven we were all present and saw the Savior chosen and appointed, and the plan of salvation made and we sanctioned it" (*The Words of Joseph Smith*, compiled and edited by Andrew F. Ehat and Lyndon W. Cook, [Provo, Utah: Religious Studies Center, Brigham Young University, 1980], 60).

57. See Job 23:10; Proverb 17:3; Zechariah 13:9.

58. "Waiting upon the Lord: Thy Will Be Done," *Ensign*, Nov. 2011, 72.

59. *HC* 2:181.

60. *To Draw Closer To God*, (Salt Lake City: Deseret Book Company, 1997), 115–16.

61. *CR*, Oct. 1993, 101.

62. *HC* 3:330–31.

63. *Gospel Doctrine*, (Salt Lake City: Deseret Book Company, 1986), 55.

64. See Zechariah 12:2–3; 13:7–9; 14:1–4; D&C 45:47–53.

65. *HC* 4:597.

66. *All These Things Shall Give Thee Experience*, (Salt Lake City: Deseret Book Company, 1980), 17.

67. In the volume entitled *Window of Faith: Latter-day Saint Perspectives on World History* (ed., Roy A. Prete, Provo, Utah: Religious Studies Center, Brigham Young University, 2005), Latter-day Saint scholars from various disciplines identified significant events that prepared the way for the Restoration of the gospel and eventually the taking of that message and the Church of Jesus Christ to all the world.

68. Quoted in "Reformation and Pre-Restoration," *Window of Faith: Latter-day Saint Perspectives on World History*, ed., Roy A. Prete, (Provo, Utah: Religious Studies Center, Brigham Young University, 2005), 288.

69. "Living in the Fulness of Times," *Ensign*, Nov. 2001, 4–5.

70. Orson Hyde's account of the First Vision, first published in Frankfurt, Germany, in *A Cry from the Wilderness, A Voice from the Dust of the Earth*, quoted in Milton V. Backman, Jr., *Joseph Smith's First Vision: Confirming Evidences and Contemporary Accounts*, (Salt Lake City: Bookcraft, 1971, 1980), 175.

71. *HC* 4:537.

72. See LDS Topical Guide, "Israel, Gathering of."

73. *JD* 22:205.

74. This passage refers specifically to Elijah revealing the priesthood, the sealing of families and planting in the hearts of the children the promises made to the fathers (D&C 2:1–2). However, it is also generally true of all of the Restoration of the fulness of the gospel and the Church of Jesus Christ.

75. "The Gift of Modern Revelation," *Ensign*, Nov. 1986, 79–80.

76. *HC* 4:540.

77. "Preparing for the Second Coming," *Ensign*, May 2004, 9.

78. "Counsel to Youth," *Ensign*, Nov. 2011, 19.

79. "If Ye Are Prepared Ye Shall Not Fear," *Ensign*, Nov. 2005, 62.

80. *Welfare Services Fact Sheet*—2010, The Church of Jesus Christ of Latter-day Saints. See also Matthew 25:35–36.

81. Joseph Fielding McConkie and Craig J. Ostler, *Revelations of the Restoration: A Commentary on the Doctrine and Covenants and Other Modern Revelations*, (Salt Lake City: Deseret Book, 2000), 561–62.

82. *Welfare Services Fact Sheet*—2010, The Church of Jesus Christ of Latter-day Saints.

83. "The Faith to Move Mountains," *Ensign*, Nov. 2006, 82–83.

84. Quoted in H. David Burton, "The Sanctifying Work of Welfare," *Ensign*, May 2011, 81. The emphasis on humanitarian aid did not end with the death of President Hinckley. President Thomas S. Monson

reported to the membership of the Church, "Since last we met, the Church has continued to provide much-needed humanitarian assistance in various locations around the world. In the past three months alone, humanitarian assistance has been provided in French Polynesia, Mongolia, Bolivia, Peru, Arizona, Mexico, Portugal, and Uganda, among other areas. Most recently we have assisted in Haiti and Chile following devastating earthquakes and tsunamis in those areas. We express our love to our Church members who have suffered in these disasters. You are in our prayers. We express profound gratitude to all of you for your willingness to assist with our humanitarian efforts by sharing your resources and, in many cases, your time, your talents, and your expertise.

"This year marks 25 years since our humanitarian program became part of our welfare effort. The number of individuals assisted by this program could never adequately be measured. We will always strive to be among the first on the scene of disasters, wherever they may occur" ("Welcome to Conference," *Ensign*, May 2010, 4).

85. *Deseret News*, Oct. 15, 1856, 252; quoted by Gordon B. Hinckley, "The Faith to Move Mountains," *Ensign*, Nov. 2005, 84.

86. *Ensign*, May 2011, 82.

87. *HC* 1:189.

88. *HC* 6:318–19.

89. *JD* 25:30–31.

90. *The Words of Joseph Smith*, compiled and edited by Andrew F. Ehat and Lyndon W. Cook, (Provo, Utah: Religious Studies Center, Brigham Young University, 1980), 11; spelling and punctuation standardized.

91. "Preparation for the Second Coming," *Ensign*, May 2004, 8.

92. *Faith Precedes the Miracle*, (Salt Lake City: Deseret Book Company, 1975), 256.

93. "Preparation for the Second Coming," *Ensign*, May 2004, 8.

94. Author's notes from Elder Jeffrey R. Holland fireside at a Kirtland, Ohio, stake center, Mar. 18, 2001.

95. The chapters from these prophets' books that have been associated with Armageddon include Isaiah 10 and 13, in which the destruction of Assyria and Babylon are viewed as types for Armageddon; Isaiah 34, 66; Jeremiah 25:15–38; Ezekiel 38–39; Daniel 8, 11–12; the entire books of Joel and Zephaniah; and Zechariah 12–14. Elder Bruce R. McConkie has been foremost in likening these Old Testament prophecies to the events he both saw in his lifetime and anticipated would unfold in the last days. He provided his thoughts on Armageddon in several chapters of his monumental work *The Millennial Messiah*, 448–94.

96. *The Illustrated Dictionary & Concordance of the Bible, New Revised Edition*, Geoffrey Wigoder, General Editor, (New York City: Sterling Publishing, 2005), 637.

97. References to a new heaven and a new earth in Revelation 21:1 and D&C 29:23 discuss the celestial earth after the Millennium.

98. *HC* 1:439–40.

99. *HC* 5:337. In the account of this same discourse, as recorded by James Burgess, Joseph explained, "As the lighting up of the morning or the dawning of the morning cometh from the east and shineth unto the west—So also is the comeing of the Son of Man. The dawning of the morning makes its appearance in the east and moves along gradualy so also will the comeing of the Son of Man be. it will be small at its first appearance and gradually becomes larger until every eye shall see it. Shall the Saints understand it Oh yes. Paul says so. Shall the wicked understand Oh no they attribute it to a natural cause. They will probably suppose it is two great comets comeing in contact with each other. It will be small at first and will grow larger and larger untill it will be all in a blaze so that every eye shall see it" (*The Words of Joseph Smith*, 181; spelling and punctuation in the original).

100. *The Millennial Messiah*, (Salt Lake City: Deseret Book Company, 1982), 578.

101. "Five Marks of the Divinity of Jesus Christ," *New Era*, Dec. 1980, 49–50.

102. *The Millennial Messiah*, (Salt Lake City: Deseret Book Company, 1982), 578–79.

103. *HC* 3:386–87.

104. *The Millennial Messiah*, (Salt Lake City: Deseret Book Company, 1982), 580–81.

105. *HC* 3:385–86.

106. *HC* 3:386.

107. *HC* 4:207–08.

108. It is reasonable to suppose that soon after the Savior's Resurrection, Adam was also resurrected.

109. *HC* 4:208–09.

110. *JD* 15:137.

111. *HC* 1:189.

112. *HC* 1:359.

113. See Craig James Ostler, "Salt Lake City: Founded Upon the Doctrine and Covenants," and "Salt Lake City: City Stake of Zion," *Salt Lake City: The Place Which God Prepared*, (Provo, Utah: Religious Studies Center, Brigham Young University, 2001), 7–25, 324–29.

114. *HC* 1:189.

115. "Becoming the Pure in Heart," *Ensign*, May 1978, 80–81.

116. *The Millennial Messiah*, (Salt Lake City: Deseret Book Com 1982), 577–78.

117. *JD* 11:16.

118. *The Words of Joseph Smith*, compiled and edited by Andrew F. Eh Lyndon W. Cook, (Provo, Utah: Religious Studies Center, B Young University, 1980), 242.

119. Ibid., 239.

120. Ibid., 233.

121. *Doctrinal New Testament Commentary*, Vol. 3, (Salt Lake C Bookcraft, Inc., 1973), 3:491.

122. For more than a century, those who were ordained to the office of a Seventy were not numbered as they served in stakes throughout the Church, and there was not even one quorum of Seventy organized. Today *none* of the Quorums of Seventy have seventy members. Neither did they wait for a quorum to fill with seventy members before they organized second, third, fourth, fifth, etc., quorums of Seventy.

123. *Opening the Seven Seals: The Visions of John the Revelator*, (Salt Lake City: Deseret Book Company, 1991), 83.

124. *HC* 6:365.

125. *HC* 5:337. The walls of present-day Old Jerusalem were built by Suleiman in 1540. The Prophet Joseph Smith foretold that the walls of Jerusalem will need to be rebuilt before the Savior appears to the Jewish remnant. It is very possible that he may have referred to the building of other walls. The Old City of Jerusalem will possibly yet be expanded to include the original city of David in an area south of the current walls. It may be that the Prophet Joseph Smith saw the wall that divides much of the current West Bank from the state of Israel. Further, the current walls may be destroyed and then rebuilt. We will simply need to await future developments to better understand the meaning and fulfillment of his statement.

David B. Galbraith, D. Kelly Ogden, Andrew C. Skinner, *Jerusalem: the Eternal City*, (Salt Lake City: Deseret Book Company, 1996), 356.

Doctrinal New Testament Commentary, 3 Vol., (Salt Lake City: Bookcraft, Inc., 1973), 1:656.

The Millennial Messiah, (Salt Lake City: Deseret Book Company, 1982), 228–29.

. Various prophecies recorded in the Old Testament make apparent allusion to these two prophets, and the Apostle John saw in vision the latter-day ministry of two witnesses in the city of Jerusalem. (See Isaiah 51:19–20; Zechariah 4:11–14; Revelation 11:1–14.)

130. *Doctrinal New Testament Commentary*, 3 Vol., (Salt Lake City: Bookcraft Inc, 1973), 3:509–10; *The Millennial Messiah*, (Salt Lake City: Deseret Book Company, 1982), 390.

131. *Doctrinal New Testament Commentary*, 3 Vol., (Salt Lake City: Bookcraft Inc, 1973), 3:510.

132. David B. Galbraith, D. Kelly Ogden, Andrew C. Skinner, *Jerusalem: the Eternal City*, (Salt Lake City: Deseret Book Company, 1996), 327.

133. *The Illustrated Dictionary & Concordance of the Bible, New Revised Edition*, ed., Geoffrey Wigoder, (New York: Sterling Publishing, 2005), 986.

134. *HC* 5:136.

ABOUT THE AUTHOR

 CRAIG JAMES OSTLER HAS BEEN a religious educator for more than thirty-five years—the first fifteen years with seminaries and institutes and the last twenty-plus years at Brigham Young University as a professor of Church history and doctrine. During that time, he has gained a well-deserved reputation as a scholar of the scriptures who has doctrinal depth and breadth. He is the author of many articles and books, including the highly acclaimed *Revelations of the Restoration: A Commentary on the Doctrine and Covenants and Other Modern Revelations*, which he coauthored with Joseph Fielding McConkie.

Craig and his wife, Sandy, are the parents of seven children and have eight grandchildren and counting. They and their family have lived in Jerusalem twice (in 1998 and again in 2008) while Dr. Ostler taught at the BYU Jerusalem Center for Near Eastern Studies. He has taught BYU Continuing Education classes for adults and BYU Education Week and has enjoyed serving as a guide to Church history sites and in the Holy Land many times over. He has served in the Church on a General Church Curriculum Writing Committee, as a bishop, as high counselor three times, and as teacher a myriad of times. He and his wife make their home in Pleasant Grove, Utah.